inside design

inside design

by michael greer

illustrated with 124 pages of photographs, 24 in full color

doubleday & company, inc., garden city, new york

contents

inside design

Whether or not you have much money to spend, but especially if you haven't, you need one marvelous decorative object which you love outrageously, which you may have spent far more for than you could afford, and perhaps which no one else in his right mind would ever have spent as much for as you did. It can be anything—a painting or a bust or an inkwell or a rug or a vase or a first folio of Shakespeare as well as a piece of furniture—located perhaps not in the most conspicuous place in the house, but surely in one that shows it off. Sometimes a pièce de résistance can be inherited, but this takes a major stroke of luck because most inherited objects must be discarded. Or it conceivably might be a bargain "find," although few finds still remain unfound. At any rate, whatever it is and whatever means are necessary to get it, you cannot resist it. What you do if your fancy seizes upon the Mona Lisa or the Sphinx at Giza I don't know, but the rule of thumb about pièces de résistance is that you have to have them. The beauty and value of the pièce de résistance may be far out of proportion to anything else you own, though in time one might hope to reduce the disparity. When you feel genuine intimations of pièce de résistanceness at a shop or gallery, buy, for there is no greater tragedy than to decide to buy later and find the pièce de résistance already bought. It's too bad

8 when the **pièce de résistance** is so big that it detracts from the setting, but that's life; the pièce de résistance, like a brown-eyed gene, tends to have its own dominant way.

Queen Anne, a girl about as diffident toward decorating as Pansy Yokum, had very little if not absolutely nothing to do with Queen Anne. She was neither interested nor influential in the creation of the style bearing her name, developed during the salad years of the eighteenth century, which saw the beginnings of many trends destined to blossom into full-fledged movements. The entire philosophy of the period was predicated upon the elongated and attenuated S scroll or reverse curve, which appears in almost every part of almost every piece if not in every of every. Before the Baroque got carried away with it this curve was a thing of beauty and a joy forever; here was lightness, elegance, and simplicity, but nervous. It quickly became clear that mahogany was the wood to watch, and the cabriole, swelling at the knee and tapering at the ankle, the leg. Wallpaper enjoyed spectacular success during the period, and very distinctive wallpaper at that. But I doubt that any grand jury will indict you if you don't

10   use Queen Anne wallpaper with **queen anne** furniture.

No cloud, however stormy, fails to have a silver lining, however hidden. And one of the blessings tucked in among the many short cuts and short shrifts builders indulge in today, the quicker to line their purses with silver, is the extinction of the picture molding. This biological sport has always been in the way—a superfluous horizontal line at just the right place to lower the ceiling—and made more of an active nuisance by hanging pictures from it like trapezes. But, as I say, the baby has been thrown out with the bath water, and among the **12 essential architectural moldings** which have all but vanished with the picture molding are cornices and (proper) baseboards. Unless one compromises with a wallpaper border at the point where wall meets ceiling, a cornice may not fail to occur. And while baseboards are rarely utterly omitted, they have suffered grave miscarriages of justice. A baseboard should be four to six inches high. It should not be embellished with a quarter-round molding at the top as though you were trying to apologize for its being there, but left flat and square. For some reason, clients are ethnically disposed to resist making budget available for essential architectural moldings; shortsighted of them. Appropriate cornice (two to five inches deep) and baseboard can both be installed in an average room for less than $100, if one can remain content with stock material. A stock installation is better than none.

Presumably you don't wish to electrocute your guests, decoratively speaking, but you certainly should wish to be interesting—even outrageous—enough to shock them a little here and there. Even when the surprise value of the shock wears off, as of course it quickly must for the owner of the shock, it can, if adroitly brought off, have a continuing what-the-hell quality pleasant to live with indefinitely. Because we daren't admit any monsters to our rooms to provide shock in themselves, but only beautiful things, we are forced to count for our shocks upon unlikely juxtapositions—of color, scale, or objects. It's a shock to see ormolu that's the quintessence of elegance on a rude Louis XVI country bureau plat. And another shock to serve the bureau plat with a crashingly contemporary institutional-type chair. The flat tailored restraint **14** of Roman shades can be a milder kind of **shock** in an opulent room where you'd surely expect elaborate and luxurious curtain treatment. Mild or violent, legitimate shocks (those neither ugly nor grotesque) are as essential as spice to stew, and to permit none of them to occur is to sign an affidavit to one's lack of imagination, wit, adjustment, or humor.

An authentic Louis XVI room has, to contemporary taste, far too much icing and far too little cake. Such a room might be either gold and white with important and abundant architectural details like dadoes, pilasters, cornices, or moldings, or a delicately pastel-painted place, choked with arabesques and garlands and bows and flowers; all of it as busy, and cloying, **16** as a piece for several harpsichords. However **louis xvi** furniture, plucked from its fussy and formal natural habitat, is something else again. Perhaps no other furniture (except Chinese or Directoire) looks so good in so many settings of other periods, mixed or matched. You can identify any period by one of its well-turned legs, and Louis XVI legs are always straight, either round or square in cross-section, often diminishing in thickness from top to bottom, and almost invariably fluted. Death was preferable to the cabriole. The whole production was cheered on if not ringmistressed by Marie Antoinette, the Madame de Pompadour of her day, whose flair took precedence over her intelligence, which was fine. Just as Napoleon wished to look different from Louis XVI and Marie, Marie wished to look different from Louis XV and Pompadour. Besides endorsing straight lines and mechanical curves, she muted fashionable colors to delicate pastels, and created a vogue for printed and painted fabrics, especially cottons in delicate narrow stripes which Napoleon later swiped and widened. Empire aped the classic. But Louis XVI was merely influenced by classicism in its search for elegance.

Nothing prevents anyone from tastefully using several floral patterns in the same place as long as there is enough difference in color and scale among them to establish their difference at a glance. Few women dislike floral patterns—or like any other category of pattern so much—which adds up to making them the world's favorite by default. (However, while using real flowers in a room naturally does not require the existence of a lady of the house, use of floral patterns in decoration almost always does.) **floral patterns** may appear printed, woven, painted, carved, or embossed, but in no case should the pattern or execution contradict the characteristic delicacy of the flower as a natural form. Over-scale roses and other flowers the size of bowling balls, when flung over floors of commercial hotels, may be grudgingly accepted by traveling salesmen, but in houses they are Victorian at best, which isn't very good, and all right only if the house is too. I don't like them anyway—they make me think of chubby cherubs or the over-weight ladies of Rubens.

18

Beyond piping a few helpful hints relating to specifics like lamp shades (never overscale) or chandeliers (never underscale) or valances (never make them too deep) nobody can

20 promulgate a gospel of **scale** because it's all bound up subjectively in taste and judgment. But you can talk around scale a little bit: (a) scale of furnishings must permit, if not encourage, maximum potential use of a room; (b) one or two startlingly overscaled (or even startlingly underscaled) pieces can enliven a setting otherwise in consistent scale, but only if they are intrinsically interesting themselves and not just big or small; (c) a room full of underscaled furniture makes people look gross and overscaled and a room full of overscaled furniture makes them look puny and underscaled, like Gulliver; (d) symmetrical balance tends to be restful and duller, asymmetrical balance nervous and more interesting; (e) overscaled objects can be shrunk by upholstering or painting them in the predominating color of the room or in a prim stripe, and underscaled ones enlarged with gushy prints or extroverted contrasting paint, but whether a given article is over or underscaled depends as much on its context as on itself; (f) sometimes a whisper can accomplish more than a shout scalewise, but you never know when till you see it; (g) the untrained eye is as offended by improper scaling as the trained, just as trained and untrained ears alike are jangled by discord, but without knowing quite what's wrong.

Among the favorite toys of many adults are stairs. Duplex—even triplex—apartments rent for the prices they do because people would perversely rather have the same amount of space split between two or among three floors and connected by **22 stairs** than all on one floor. Even a single step or two seems to count, and I think they are secretly responsible for the success of such absurdities as raised dining areas and conversation pits, the latter a term I can scarcely bring myself to articulate let alone immortalize. Stairs are irresistible fun, apparently, both to look at and to go up and down; an opera house without stairs for the audience to show itself off is unthinkable. Little flights of stairs in residences take on an integrity and éclat far out of proportion to their net worth when curved. Uncarpeted stairs are less luxurious, noisier, and more perilous than carpeted ones. Carpets on stairs should be specially woven, their borders designed with any idiosyncrasies of the particular steps in mind, and held in place with brass bars, as they are in Europe but rarely are here.

Crystal, the jewelry of interior decoration, finds its way so often into lamps, chandeliers, and sconces because both the **crystal** and the light benefit from the interplay between them as light passes through the prisms, baguettes, and balls. Crystal is what you make it—dazzling in elaborate chandeliers, chaste and pristine in single-column lamps (the only bad things about which are that the wire must be exposed, and that nobody knows how to make them any more the way they did in the eighteenth and nineteenth centuries). As nonilluminating accessories—ash trays, boxes, vases, and decanters —crystal is the most catholic of all materials, safe even to give as wedding presents because it looks as though it was intended from the very start to be a part of any setting it happens to land in. But whatever its incarnation, the simpler and less ornamented each individual piece can be—whether complete in itself or one of many crystal components in a complicated chandelier—the better. Crystal can be man-made or God-made; the latter is usually less crystal clear, but otherwise, if the quality and design are equal, equally desirable.

Ephemeral though they may be, flowers must be chosen and arranged with as much care as though they were permanent. They must complement the scheme and not cause a color conflict. They should also be arranged so carefully that they seem not really to be arranged at all. Florists, especially, do badly at flower arrangements. There are formal and informal flower arrangements (informal ones look lovely in formal settings, and formal ones should be attempted only by those few who can bring them off without the look of being arranged —almost an impossibility), and formal (lilies) and informal (daisies) flowers too. You can't make a tulip look formal, nor a daffodil, nor an anemone, although anemones are both informal and sophisticated. If you wish to create a color accent, only one kind and color of flower should appear in any container; otherwise, tasteful mixtures are welcome. Propaganda: that stems have intrinsic worth, and that the longer they are the better. Nonsense. Most of the time they should be snipped down, although there is some justification for long-stemmed roses in a room with ceiling of imposing height. The classical Japanese arrangement with perhaps two-thirds of the stem out and one-third in the container is all right if you want a classical oriental arrangement, and not if you don't, and I don't. Too many **flowers** in a room imply the presence of a corpse and should be avoided unless there is one, and even then too many flowers can distress anyone of delicate taste.

27

America's universally favorite color seems to be black (no color at all, of course) and its second favorite white (no color either). There is scarcely a room in America without some black in it; often not much, but invariably some; an interior of a house without it is as rare as the interior of a woman's closet without a little black dress. Black (by itself or contrasted with white) is dramatic and elegant and a faithful foil for other colors of all kinds and intensities, subtle to pyrotechnical. The play of black on other blacks of different sheens and tactilities can beat Scheherazade at sensuousness. Imagine the ravishing effect of a room with black velvet or black lacquered or black flocked wallpapered walls, a black polished hardwood floor, upholstered pieces covered in black textured tweed against exposed fruitwood, a table surface or so in black marble or black Carrara glass, and perhaps a mir-

28 ror **black** lamp, moldings of black lacquer, and black marbleized baseboards—all of it relieved of course with non-black objects and splashes of color, e.g., a throw of matched baby jaguars, and perhaps the glint of steel. Women are their most radiant in black rooms; even men muster a glow. While in practice it is almost impossible to get carried away with black if you relieve and accent it, the thought of an orgy of black terrifies the lay imagination. Too bad. But certainly a little more than a little black, like classical Chinese, belongs everywhere. The black telephone is becoming extinct and chic.

Family rooms somewhat atone for their unavoidably low decorative station by at least serving as catchall for all the trappings which, if they weren't confined to the family room, would be off helping to ruin some other part of the house. Here, if they must be somewhere, and combined into one, are bar, dance hall, music room, casino, and assembly point or parade ground for all the various accoutrements of contemporary American life we feel compelled to own and use— movie projectors and television sets and electric organs et al. In colonial America the family room was—and sometimes it still is—the kitchen, but the various family props these days are becoming so numerous that, if only out of compassion for the cook, the family should go appropriate another room. Obviously the family room has to be what you might call "thoroughly" designed in order to incorporate the diverse matters of interest to any family cohabiting in harmony.

30 I wish **family rooms** didn't have to be called family rooms, but this or anything is better than calling them Florida, Texas, or California rooms—asinine as calling a pea a garden pea, as menus of restaurants along throughways do.

32 A small room with wallpapered walls can be made to seem larger and more unified by **wallpapering the ceiling** with the same paper as the walls. Bold directional patterns may prudently be avoided when papering ceilings, since anarchy will occur where the direction of the ceiling wallpaper runs at right angles to the direction of the wall wallpaper, as it must in two cases of the available four. Muted directional patterns can be satisfactory, but the direction should flow across the ceiling and down the most conspicuous wall, usually the one which confronts you upon entry (and, through the nature of things, its opposite mate, the wall which confronts you upon exit). Striped wallpaper is an exception; pleasant tent-like effects can be achieved by mitring the ceiling paper so that the stripes run at right angles to the wall stripes at all four walls. I have never papered a ceiling in anything but the paper used for the walls; I can see no point in ceiling paper which defeats the purpose of ceiling paper. Amateurs try to judge a wallpaper pattern by pinning up a couple of panels and imagining the total effect, an impossibility for the untrained eye. Clients should be barred from rooms while wallpapering is in progress, in order to resolve doubts about choice of pattern and perhaps, after second thought, to halt work. There would be more to undo if the client decided against the pattern upon seeing the fully papered room, but this hasn't occurred in my own experience.

Tôle, a term which may be applied to any painted metal, can bring charm, warmth, and unobtrusive gaiety to any room, even the most severely elegant. Tôle is informal in intrinsic attitude, yet Louis XIV scattered it here and there about Versailles, and I have yet to create a room without recommending at least one tôle object. The best antique examples date from the late seventeenth century through the early nineteenth century, and include trays, teapots, jardinieres, candlesticks, vases, oil lamps, chandeliers, boxes, and limitless small accessories. Popular ground colors, finished with mellow and durable glazes, were sealing-wax red, mustard yellow, olive green, and black, all often decorated with gold. If you are lucky enough to find a good orange, blue, white, tortoise shell, or mica tôle piece while browsing in an English or French country shop, disguise your interest and obliquely inquire the price. France and England produced most of the antique tôle; the Italians for some reason remained unfascinated. There is some crude American tôle, which can be charming. Contemporary tôle sold today in department stores

—though surely **tôle** by definition—is uniformly terrible.

It is almost always more diverting to look through something at something than just to look at something. Looking through a window at the outdoors is better than looking at the outdoors outdoors. The same is true indoors. You can create **36** bona fide **look through** with architectural embellishments, like arches, or mere arrangements which direct the eye between them, like combinations of plants, curtains, screens, or tall pieces of furniture. Look through can be trompe l'oeil, as can anything. Look through, or at least the means necessary to create look through, can serve double duty by hiding ugly structural encroachments. Another double duty function is to set off part of a room to use for a different purpose from the rest of the room, like eating or sleeping. Dramatized door openings make highly satisfactory look through, especially when assisted by floors of outspoken design which continue right through the opening from one area to another. The window-display man is luckier than the interior designer because everything he does has the advantage—the eternal mystery and fascination—of look through. So does the theater set designer. Even the man frying eggs in the window of the short-order food shop gathers crowds; not because he's frying eggs, but because he's doing it in the window. Vital to the success of any look through is making sure that there is something interesting beyond for the eye to look at once it has looked through. Somebody must always be frying the egg.

When a Chinese ornaments or decorates an object in classical Chinese fashion the result is Chinese; when a westerner does so, it's chinoiserie. Chinoiserie refers to ornamentation and not silhouette; when silhouette is imitated you have imitation Chinese, not chinoiserie. The art of chinoiserie flourished at fad intensity during the time of the English Regency—it was a new and amusing thing to do—had a hiatus during the Directoire and Empire periods, but is once again booming **38** today. Much of the charm of **chinoiserie** lies in the fact that the artist (a) doesn't succeed in accurately copying the real McCoy and (b) doesn't want to anyway. The subtly stylized result often has more wit and more variety of color than authentic Chinese. The seemingly miscegenetic marriage of, say, a pure Louis XVI escritoire and chinoiserie ornamentation has unimpeachable integrity; yet it discreetly amuses as it satisfies, which is just about all you can ask of anything.

40 biographical acknowledgments are unique among decorative objects in the sense that what is fitting and proper for one person can be quite unfitting and improper for another, depending upon the biography. They may range from the obvious—a continuously exposed typewriter, unabridged dictionary, and an arrangement of his collected works in the home of a writer; to the subtle—perhaps a painting painted by the mistress of the house. Musical instruments and collections of all kinds, tools or products of many intellectually admirable arts, even filing cabinets, can count. The personal link to the owner—the acknowledgment of his vocation or avocation—lifts almost everything, sometimes even paintings which a stranger would surely burn, to the stature of a bona fide decorative object. Even mounted heads of animals shot by the master (if not malevolent in expression), stuffed fish hooked by him, models of ships made by him have their place provided the rooms in which they are displayed are wisely chosen. Sops to the ego and family memorabilia, apostrophes to, or remembrances of, glories past, such as coats of arms and framed letters from former heads of state, belong in the family's private rooms and should never be flaunted before guests. Academic degrees, certificates of discharge and documentations of intellectual, public, self-sacrificing, or sustained achievements are better hung at the office where they won't irritate already enlightened members of the household at home, and can impress or reassure professional associates.

Chairs with caned backs and seats not only look, but are, cooler to lean against and sit on, but to protect the caning from wearing through as quickly as it almost does anyway, I usually put an upholstered hair pad on the seat. One instantly recognizes hand caning, infinitely superior to machine caning, by its being laced into the frame of a chair; edges of machine caning are hidden under a strip of molding in the hope of concealing its low origin—the vain hope as it turns out because the mere presence of such moldings is as revealing as it is concealing. Traditional caning patterns are built around the octagonal hole, but some contemporary manufacturers are producing a perfectly honorable square-holed pattern for chairs and cabinet doors. Besides being a refreshing change in **42** a roomful of upholstered backs **caning** amounts to fully accredited look through. I prefer to allow caned chairs to stand free in the room rather than against a wall where there is nothing to look through them at. Painting caning is always a risk; any sensitive eye agrees that for cane the color of natural cane is not improved upon but usually only detracted from.

Books are to furnish the house as well as the mind, customarily the former. Books with fine leather bindings are beautiful objects, and books without fine leather bindings but with colorful paper jackets make an important contribution too. But contemporary "sets" of books in the various "library" series can better be read and discarded, or stored out of sight. A number of decorators, usually women, have fallen into the habit of slipcovering books in papers of colors drawn from the rest of the room; no one can tell whether slipcovered books are really blocks of lumber or bricks, which in some cases I have discovered them to be. Books with particularly beautiful covers deserve to be faced forward on the shelves. Buying books by the linear yard may be deplored by the academicians, but it's better than leaving shelves barren; when doing so, I try to pick titles which could conceivably be of interest to the client eventually, if not now. Provided their bookshop jackets happen to pick up part of the color scheme itself, hot-off-the-press books of sufficient notoriety to turn up in cocktail party conversation can be attractive decorative accessories when just left "casually" lying about. This may seem a frivolous detail, though it is not. When you see a best-seller with a red jacket lying on a lacquered table of the same shade of red (or equivalent) the impression is hard to resist that the jacket itself was somehow designed with your room in mind. But when **books** with color-scheme jackets are more than a very few months old it looks as though you're either late or trying.

45

In a baroque piece, as in a German band, a great many things are probably going on at once. Asymmetrical swirls and scrolls and whorls and whirls fling themselves abandonedly into, onto, around, and through each other, for an effect of flamboyance which, typically, at least flirts with being just too too much. Baroque elicits ambivalence in most tasteful people today. A piece or two of it in a setting monitored by a lot of cool and collected furniture that doesn't panic easily may be effective, but the mélange must be dished up with care. Baroque really is crudely worked, overscaled, and undisciplined, if not frenzied, Louis XV before Louis XV—or his court—got hold of it; all the right curves and cabrioles are **46** there, but in gross welter and profusion. **rococo** distilled the nectar from baroque, but the Victorian period fell simply for its excess for the sake of excess and piled on even further excess to create freaks more ghastly than even atomic radiation of the baroque chromosomes could have produced.

Whatever you do, you can't let a window or windowed door or group of either simply stop at the top without some kind of tying together or acknowledgment even if it's just a horizontal pole from which curtains hang on rings. Window treatments often call for valances, yet today you'd hardly think so because practically everybody seems to have lost his sense of valance. Of course, one excuse for not using a valance is to use a cornice, but it's hard to find a legitimate reason for using neither (as when French doors, which open in, wouldn't, if valanced or corniced, open at all). Just as I am unjustly accused of pinheadedness in my correctly scaled lampshades, I am accused of shallowness in my valances; yet the only **48 valances** which can properly be deeper than one and a half inch for each foot of ceiling height are Victorian ones in a pure Victorian setting. My own preference runs to festooned valances, with soft folds of fabric, and to scalloped ones, always buckram lined and never mounted on plywood, which is appropriate—if ever—only in hotels, offices, and institutions content with compromise. Tufted valances are an abomination. Sometimes it is possible in high-ceilinged rooms to use a valance (always fabric, either identical or in contrast to the curtain material) under a cornice (often covered in the valance fabric) without appearing to pile Pelion upon Ossa.

50 People who work in **offices** spend more presumably waking time in them than they do in their houses, and hence the recent sweep of attention to office interior design is long over-due and sensible. Also sensible: to have the same interior designer who did a person's house do his office because, pro-vided of course the house is a success, the rapport essential between client and designer can be in no doubt; to bar the wife (or husband) of the occupant of the office from confer-ences with the designer about it (the reverse of what must happen in regard to the house where both parties should be present at all planning discussions); to assure the office's being functional and pleasant, but beyond that to make it look as much like an office or a room in a house or any com-promise between the two as the client cares; and to encourage a radically different mood or atmosphere in the office from that which exists at home, merely for spice of life's sake. Changes of pace per se are even more effective in offices than in houses because you somehow expect them less. I enjoyed importing American antiques to furnish an office in Paris; the French client was, and remains, astonished and pleased.

The effect of hand-painted murals can be honorably duplicated with scenic wallpaper at less cost, unless, of course, the scenic wallpaper, instead of being printed, is hand-painted too. Scenic papers (and murals) enlarge the room with their perspectives and provide a continuing design more interesting because it is nonrepetitive. You can easily find scenic paper which continues through scene after different scene for sixty feet or more before the repeat occurs, by which time you have most likely forgotten the earlier appearance of the scene anyway (if the room is even large enough to permit a repeat). The most interesting or dominant scene should be applied to the most conspicuous wall area. This done, the other scenes should be allowed to occur as they happen to, though it helps the composition if you can do a little juggling to achieve height—perhaps via a building or a mountain or a tree—at architectural interruptions like doors or terminations of walls, and here trompe l'oeil painting can come in handy to patch and match. Scenic papers do not wish to have pictures hanging on them, and if there must be a mirror it should cover that part of the paper of most incidental interest. Some scenics can be hung to the baseboard, but most were, and are, printed to go from ceiling to chair rail. I use them most often in elevator vestibules, narrow halls, galleries and dining **52** rooms. Scenes from fine antique **scenic wallpapers** may properly be framed and then hung up as pictures.

Room dividers, friendly frauds, pretend to be walls without actually or completely dividing one room into two. If they did they would be honest-to-God walls and not room dividers. A room is divided against itself if the division results in a net loss of spaciousness. A fairly foolproof way to avoid this is to divide the divider into panels, each framing a mirror. Where encroachments upon space are no problem, room dividers may also be made of open or closed book-or-storage cases, or decorative panels, perhaps shoji screens, or fabric shirred on rods at top and bottom if not stretched taut. In any case **room dividers** are *non gratae* unless they are so attractive that they deserve being lived with for themselves, irrespective of disguising or dividing. A divider needn't be fastened to both floor and ceiling (though it certainly must be to at least one or the other), but if so some space must be left open at top and/or bottom or it might as well be wall after all. Whether dramatizing, concealing, or simply dividing space from space the impression conveyed must be one of permanence, not transience; structural and architectural integration with the rest of the room has to happen. Like look through, room dividers pose the eternal mystery question, what lies beyond?—a bit of a mystery even when you know.

54

I'd probably lack the moral fiber to do this to the Hope diamond or the Stone of Scone, but I not only would but have **56** cut antique **breakfronts and secretaries** more or less in half the long way, slicing them right through to make them thinner. It's easy: You remove their backs, decide how thin you want them, carefully saw them in two along their axes, put the backs back on and have breakfronts and secretaries to see you through thin instead of thick. Since much of their point is their verticality in the first place, giving them this Procrustean reducing treatment to diminish their depth and thus increase their powers of uplift can be only ethical. A secretary is meant as a desk and a breakfront as a storage unit, but otherwise both are really breakfronts, with their bottoms thicker than their tops, and their fronts broken at the point where the bottom juts out beyond the top. Don't light the interior of a breakfront unless you wish it to look like a fixture for the display of gift shop merchandise at an airline terminal. You may conceal the contents with curtains under the glass. Or, if there is no glass, show treasures off and yet protect them with wire woven in a miniature chicken-wire weave mounted on the doors. If the breakfront or secretary has a key, put a colored silk tassel on it. When/if the key falls to the floor, you'll instantly find it. And when it doesn't, you'll have a decorous little splashette of unanticipated color.

Why bore anyone with an itemization of the ten basic kinds of arches when he would then simply have to go to the trouble of forgetting them? Suffice it to say that three of the ten kinds —Moorish, Persian, and ogee—were highly admired by builders of movie palaces in the 20s and 30s, where they should forever stay until demolition do them part, and that any arches used in interior design provide the most successful possible combination of room divider and look through. As witness the Rue de Rivoli or any Roman aqueduct, arches in series are lighter, more graceful, and vertical in feeling than single arches can ever be. Now few interiors have quite the geography to work with that the Rue de Rivoli has, but **58** at least two **arches** in series are better than one, and three better than two. My own arch inclinations run to the classical and neoclassical types, particularly segmental and semi-circular and Palladian ones. But if somebody wanted a Tudor or Gothic room I suppose I would go ahead and use the Tudor or Gothic arch, and in fact have. I avoid the elliptical arch because I like compass-drawn curves better than ellipses. And flat arches, with straight sides and a horizontal member, seem arches more by definition than by appearance, like flat feet.

One of the accredited sops to a nation's ego in the innocent past, before chauvinistic status symbols graduated to the nuclear-explosion and the rocketing-of-anthropoid-into-orbit league, was to establish a porcelain factory. In the late seventeenth and early eighteenth centuries the nations of Europe were in a frenzy of formulating and stirring and glazing and firing, each in the attempt to be first with an **60** indigenous national **porcelain** roughly in imitation of, or inspired by, the porcelain or chinaware already made for centuries in the orient. Operations were cloaked in a secrecy appropriate to Oak Ridge, and judging from the tight security, the stealing of porcelain secrets may have been worthy game for international espionage. The Germans won. They put the first hard-paste Meissen (Dresden) on the market in 1713. The English, who sophisticated some of their formulas with ground-up bones, and the French followed soon after. But America languished on and on with no porcelain factory worth its salt, unable to hold up its head among nations. In 1902, President Roosevelt set out to find an American porcelain works capable of creating a domestic porcelain for the White House and could find none. Not until 1918 did the White House acquire a satisfactory dining service produced on these shores. (Nor did the White House have a room furnished entirely with American antiques of the period of the White House itself. This was corrected in 1960 by the National Society of Interior Designers, on whose behalf I presented such a room to President Eisenhower for the nation.)

Without a border on a rug you don't have a rug, you just have a piece of cloth lying there, like a towel. Without a border a rug isn't a prescribed entity, isn't official, doesn't have a passport or accrediting credentials, as it were. There are those who accomplish their borders by sewing on fringe or separately woven designs, but I like to conceive my rugs totally, border included. By their nature, borders have to amount to a linear band of width varying from rug to rug, but what goes on within the band can be any combination of stripes or designs imaginable, consistent with good taste. Patterned borders may go on rugs with plain or patterned fields. So may plain ones. **rug borders** don't have to contrast with the field in color—they can be carved or engraved or woven to contrast—but why waste the excellent opportunity to acknowledge and reinforce colors drawn from elsewhere in the scheme of the room? Speaking of rugs, there's no more ridiculous term—I suppose the invention of a gushy so-called shelter magazine—in common parlance today than "area" rugs; I defy anyone to show me any rug that doesn't cover an area. If you want to, you can find a photograph in this picture book of a rug without a border, but I dearly wish it had one, which it would if circumstances out of my control hadn't etc.

Today, when everybody knows what time it is anyway, there is no excuse for visible clocks unless they help to ornament the room in which they are visible. Shops are chock-full of beautiful antique clocks; clockmakers of certain periods, like Empire, were so compulsively fascinated with their trade that they must have worked quite round the clock to turn out the tens of thousands they turned out. Large grandfather and grandmother clocks (good because they are tall and thin for precious verticality) are appropriate for foyers, halls, and occasional rooms, but quite inhospitable in dining, sitting, and drawing rooms. Large or small, and not to tell the time but just because they ought to be, clocks should be running—hopefully making as little audible noise as possible—and it is preferable to replace old works with new than to continue to enshrine an inoperable corpse. Most antique **clocks** without pendulums run soundlessly. Gag clocks, like cuckoo ones, never amuse and never fail to reflect on the intelligence and taste of anyone displaying them; they are charming in the shadow of the Jungfrau, perhaps, but there among the cheese and chocolate they should remain. Although it may not have occurred to them, sensitive souls dislike elaborately or loudly chiming clocks; one has to train the mind not consciously to hear enough as it is without imposing this additional burden.

The Chinese traditionally like to display and dramatize fine porcelain on bases of teak or gold, but the western world developed a penchant for pedestals. The trouble was that the admiration for this classical form grew to take precedence over the quality of the objects displayed upon it, which people finally realized was absurd, and perhaps as a result of being caught in the cross fire, pedestals haven't the currency today that they ought to. Small pedestals for small ornaments can be taken or left, but sometimes pedestal tables amount to a practical necessity. For they have, patently, but one base—a relief in any room tending toward the leggy anyway, and a convenience in small, heavily trafficked areas where conventional legs would trip up passers-by. One thicker base or leg is also more architectural in feeling than four thinner ones, and the design of most pedestals goes out of its way to make it more so. Rooms of impoverished architectural interest therefore see their fortunes change at least a little for the better when a pedestal table, or with greater luck a pair of them, gets moved in. Even the simplest square or rectangular **66 pedestals** help to dramatize the importance of sculpture.

Like a fragile frigate miraculously managing to stay in one exquisite piece while riding at anchor between the Scylla of Louis XVI and the Charybdis of Empire, the Directoire period was surely influenced by its powerful neighbors, but by no means engulfed. This transitional time of the Directorate, which served as the political connecting tissue between the royal and the imperial, was a time of studied—though apparently ingenuous—simplification. Instead of going out of its way to prove a point, as all the other periods did, Directoire went out of its way not to prove a point. Instead of going all out, it went all in. Flagrant spending was both out of fashion and out of the question. If you had to sum up the **68 directoire** in a sentence, as you wouldn't wish to do, you might say that here was the floatingness of Louis XVI with the neoclassicism of Empire with the fussiness of neither. Stripped even of its fluting, furniture floated as never before or since. The fine French hand, which now devoted itself entirely to line without ornamental distractions, achieved a classicism of its own. Because expensive wood was expensive, paint and lacquer often covered inexpensive woods, always with understatement. What little ornament there was was understated too—everything was the plainest of geometry— the mechanically drawn straight line, arc, rectangle, lozenge. Provincial and town furniture could scarcely be told apart. Directoire is all quintessence. There is little matter of degree.

Glazing walls, instead of merely painting them, is no mere vainglorious extravagance because, under their varnish, **70 glazed walls** last perhaps half a dozen times longer. So, of course, in the long run they are both less expensive and more elegant, strange bedfellows today or ever. First a wall is painted. Then the glaze goes on; it may match or contrast with the color of the paint, but either way you get a two-color effect because before the glaze is dry it is attacked with brush and cheesecloth to produce one of three effects: strie, stippled, or mottled, the latter rather passé. The strie effect is the most tempting because the "graining" suggests wood, and simply by indicating paneling through application of molding to a plaster wall and glazing the whole business you have a beautiful bargain boiserie. A buttermilk glaze, which happens when buttermilk is painted onto the walls at the proper moment in the glazing, results in a fascinating thick-coated look reminiscent of antique paint, and a perennial conversational gambit.

No one has to be told that mirrors achieve space—depth, height, and perspective—and that they can create pleasant repeats of color and design. Also, looking at something in a mirror is better than just looking at something—a state of affairs analogous to the effect of trompe l'oeil. Mirrors should preferably be opposite windows in rooms having but one window wall. They should never be located where anyone has to sit facing smack into them, for then they become a distraction and nuisance. Mirrors must, categorically, be framed. Antique mirrors are apt to be in two parts because there was a limit to the size of pre-nineteenth century glass. Trumeaux are French

72 mirrors with an overdecoration (a carving or painting or panel of applied gesso or bronze doré or tôle); such mirrors were built right into or onto boiseries which is why you often see them surrounded by a recessed wood "frame," cut, upon removal of the mirror, from the living paneling itself. Trumeaux are wonderful over mantels, because of their importance. Most people in their heart of hearts loathe tinted mirrors, like pink ones which lull them into a false security instantly shattered by the very next untinted mirror they look into, that much worse if it's in the same house. The only competition for a mirror is a painting, which has to be pretty good to beat the mirror. Mirrors give windows a run for their money. Walls of mirrors I like only in halls or elevator vestibules or other little areas through which one passes only intermittently or quickly.

Ever since Pandora—and maybe even before—people have been fascinated by boxes as decorative objects, whether or not they know what's in them. Boxes don't have to have particular intrinsic worth to justify their use in decoration. Most old boxes of any kind, even so low in estate as cigar boxes, turn out to be attractive, probably because people can't bear to throw away a pretty box, or to keep an ugly one. Some situations all but require boxes; for example, a box provides an ideal horizontal element to tie the picture or mirror above the mantel to the mantel, and also fill the gap between the ornaments on each end. Even boxes which perform menial chores like holding coal or kindling must also earn their keep by their looks. Nobody uses tea caddies for tea parties any more—these make fine holders for smoking apparatus on cocktail tables. All the unattractive little items from the notion department that you have to have handy but don't want to look at all the

74 time should go into **boxes** (or drawers) placed near the place you're most likely to need them. The only instance I can think of in which a box should not be used as an operating box is when it is used as a table base under a plate-glass top. I don't think it's too neurotic to keep the telephone in an antique box.

Window hangings, properly called curtains, may also be called draperies but never drapes. A drape can only be an individual draped element within a curtain treatment and never the whole thing. Curtains for windows, walls, and beds evolved as utilitarian means to ends of warmth and privacy, but soon became **76** decorative ends in themselves. Crucial to **curtains** are linings, and I wish I had a doubloon for every argument I've had insisting that curtains not only be lined with sateen, if not silk, but interlined with flannel. No treatment less dedicated produces such opulent folds, prevents unwanted light from sifting through and revealing the inner construction, and lengthens the life and protects the color of the curtains as well. Where architecture permits I like to do a triple-threat curtain treatment. First, stationary curtains of, perhaps, silk damask. Then, under them, draw curtains, maybe of silk taffeta. And then under them a third set, sheer undercurtains—the things most people think are curtains—to diffuse the light and provide a screen of privacy during the day. Labor to make proper curtains runs neck and neck with the cost of the materials and sometimes exceeds it. But there is nothing to do but pay not pray, for poorly tailored curtains, like poorly tailored couturier originals, amount to a waste of fabric. Curtains are the preferable term, but I sometimes lose my nerve and substitute draperies—more substantial and important sounding—in estimates which might otherwise bring on a client apoplexy.

78 Antique **painted furniture** usually looks better than contemporary painted furniture simply because—and this is of course true of other antiques—few or no craftsmen today can acceptably imitate it. Italians generally, and provincial artists of all western countries, have always been addicted to painted furniture, though no rule can be promulgated which confines it to informal settings. Only the color and design of the individual piece indicate where it may go. Even gaily painted pieces may look right in otherwise parochial formal settings if the detailing is elaborate or delicate or refined enough. I often use an important, painted high cabinet as the focal point of interest in a strictly formal room which has no fireplace or other striking architectural element. Versailles had many light, airy and colorful painted pieces which looked fine because they were ornamented so exquisitely. Paint always relieves a room full of a lot of naturally finished wood and upholstered pieces, particularly if there is much mass or bulk to them. Old paint, even when in "poor" condition, should usually not be condemned to restoration. Just as wrinkles often contribute character to a face, chipped and worn paint often brings beauty to the piece which it never owned when young.

The place to start, in designing any interior, is with color. Colors must be sorted into three categories: those the client can't bear, those it can, and those it prefers. Since the wrong (for you) colors can drive you as surely crazy as Chinese water torture, color is the first consideration chronologically and the first in total importance as well. The unfailing omission of colors agonizing to the person whose interior it is is more important than the inclusion of colors enthusiastically admired. Color cannot be merely discussed or disaster will occur; color must be shown in chips or swatches or paint samples. No one should be influenced by anyone in his choice of color, certainly never by his friends who, where color is concerned, are enemies. But a qualified designer is equipped to ferret out and analyze what somebody's color preferences actually are—which may be a far cry from what he thinks or says they are (favorite colors in clothes are often not, strangely enough, what turn out to be favorite colors in an interior). Successful color depends upon juxtaposition too, and a loathed color can become loved if used in exciting or soothing context. There are no "decorator" colors because all colors have probably existed forever, and surely for millennia before the creation of the first decorator. But there are decorator combinations of colors, and here lies the interior designer's most crucial creative contribution. Color is the first thing you're aware of in any room, because it takes precedence over period, design, arrangement, and quality. Color is never merely color, but instant **color**. **81**

The best way to entice casual guests into impromptu bridge games is to have a permanent gaming installation so inviting that to stay and play looks like more fun than either to stay or leave and not play. Essentials (besides potable refreshments) to **gaming installations**: Skillfully handled lighting. Chairs which look and are comfortable to sit in for protracted periods. And a table surface pleasant to play on and look extendedly down at; my suggestions are leather or felt.

82

One of middle class America's bugaboos is that walls have some kind of sacred cow divinity and must not have too many—if any—picture nails driven into them. How ridiculous, when you can drive enough nails into a wall to make a respectable fakir's bed, pull them out, and make the wall as good as new with just a couple of dabs of plaster and paint. So it is not out of veneration for walls that I sometimes display paintings standing loose on easels. The fact is that most paintings look their best when slanting slightly backward, for this was their position as the artist painted them—and when viewed at their originally painted height. (Frank Lloyd Wright wanted paintings at the Guggenheim to lean backward but too many of the canvases were too big to do so against the concave walls.) Not only can paintings be moved from easel to easel around the house for variety, but the easels can be moved from place to place too. Easels must be in scale with the paintings they display and attractive objects in themselves—if they're not I'm **84** likely to upholster them in velvet. Little table-size **easels** may decoratively display china. Antique music stands make wonderful easels for small pictures or framed drawings. Orientals are enormously fond of moving lovely decorations about the house to experience them under a range of conditions, and of putting them away and taking them out again to savor their absence and return. Easels encourage this admirable practice.

Italian furniture periods correspond to French periods in time, product, and name. Thus we have Italian Louis XVI, Italian Directoire, Italian Empire, et al. The Italians turned out their furniture with by no means a finer, but rather a more hot-blooded or gay, hand than the French. They loved fruit wood and they loved paint and gilt. They decked out a good deal of what they made in carnival colors. They liked to trim with gold, and often lost control of themselves and merrily gilded an entire piece (as I must admit so did the French but somehow **86** more conservatively). **italian furniture**, worked with less patience, is usually a little cruder and less classic in proportion, for all its joie de vivre. The French might grumpily labor over the detailing of the bombe front of a commode for weeks, but the Italians preferred to glue something together quick, slap their extroverted color and gilt on it, forget it, and go gaily on to something else in high good humor.

88 pianos should fit easily into residential rooms and not be dramatically posed or poised as if Liszt were about to spring from behind an arras and rip off a rhapsody. The shape of the grand piano is above reproach. But even upright ones are highly admirable, their often ugly or indifferently attractive silhouettes completely excused by the fact that they are pianos. Pianos must have ebony black finishes, it turns out as I review the dozens of pianos I have installed, anywhere but in play or family rooms. There, why not lacquer them white—or a high old color. Brown pianos are like brown shoes with black tie. When a pièce de résistance, any piano up to and including a concert grand may legitimately appear in almost any room, no matter how small, merely large enough to contain it, and a pox upon scale. Grand pianos should have their tops propped open all the way only when being seriously played, if then. At all other times the top must fly at half-mast. Never completely close it. This incidentally precludes shawls and other jetsam from finding their final resting places upon the piano top which, like a mantel, is otherwise an irresistible magnet for junk. If I'm not allowed to abort delivery of the piano manufacturer's matching bench, or in some way to get rid of it after arrival, I camouflage it as much as possible with a decorative pad if not an upholstered top. Otherwise a musicale to be performed by very young students of the piano seems perennially imminent.

When manipulated skillfully in decoration, bamboo manages always to be engagingly tongue in cheek while never quite bursting out laughing. Its nature is light and airy, and so should be the designing which bamboo is required to execute. Like any delicate commodity, it can be forced unwillingly into grotesque or pompous situations by a heavy hand. But encouraged in its lighthearted natural inclinations, bamboo can properly bring a sigh of relief to any room full of even dedicated and serious-minded furniture. Besides contributing successfully to furniture, bamboo—or printed or painted trompe l'oeil bamboo motifs—can be flung against walls and ceilings in fretwork trellises or other fragile arrangements to create depth, height, look through, and air. A little—and sometimes a lot—of **bamboo** can go almost anywhere, like so many things that started in China. And unlike most things that began in China or anywhere, imitation (carved wood) or interpretive (printed, painted) bamboo is as pedigreed as real.

90

When a magazine editor asked me for a name to describe my flat fabric-panel window shades, made to be raised in a straight line and gathering in straight horizontal accordion folds, I

92 decided to call them **roman shades** because I conceived the idea for them while musing over an unusual awning in Rome. The operating principle of Roman shades is identical to that of Austrian shades, but Roman ones are far more tailored and neat, without the flamboyant scalloped lushness which more and more today is the kind of treatment you expect at the windows of nationally advertised reducing salons. Roman shades can be used with formal or informal draperies, or with neither if you wish a more contemporary and less elaborate treatment. When used alone, Roman shades should have a frame, which can be even a literal picture frame kind of frame. Beyond the immaculate way they look, compelling recommendations for Roman shades are the facts that they can fall from ceiling to floor, can mask the architectural caprices which occur above and around windows particularly in recently constructed buildings, and can imply a window area—both in height and width—greater than exists. Monochromatic fabrics are effective as Roman shades, but far less than stripes (self-stripes or applied braid or tape to create stripes) or prints. Roman shades make maximum use of any pretty print because such an expanse of fabric allows for several complete repetitions of the repeat.

94 The point about concealed **built-in cupboards** to remember is simply this: like sonnets, they must both bow to the artificial limitations arbitrarily imposed upon them (in the case of the sonnet, the 14-line format; in that of built-in cupboards, concealing storage space) and, in the process, soar beyond the limitations, becoming greater art because of them. In other words, architecturally integrated and structurally co-ordinated concealed storage space, if you will excuse the Latinized mouthful, should never merely store, but should both store and look as though you would have wanted it even if you didn't want or need the storage space; either the perhaps vitally necessary utilitarian function becomes, through design, dwarfed by and incidental to the design, or the design flops. Never to interrupt or compete with the decoration of a room, and instead always to improve upon it and further its ends, isn't easy. The handling of architecturally integrated storage is the designer's nightmare and his joy. The brightest star on this particular horizon is boiserie, which often can light the path to success.

The dictionary defines an accessory as a thing which contributes subordinately, an adjunct or accompaniment not essential.

96 The dictionary errs, for **accessories** are categorically essential, at least in interior design. Moreover superior accessories can justify inferior furniture, but never vice versa. Tooth and hair might be thought of as accessories to the human head, yet people often give more thought to what's on top of their scalp than beneath, and certainly no one grins until a recently knocked-out front tooth has been replaced. Similarly, decorative accessories, which should really be called crucials, should receive a dramatic budget allocation. Accessories are the difference between reposing rooms in funeral parlors, analysts' offices, public libraries, church meeting rooms, judges' chambers, department store "model" rooms, presidential suites in hotels, etc., and a room you could bear to take a breath in. Accessories are like a man's close shave or a woman's lipstick—little in themselves but devastating in their absence. They can be to use and look at (lamps, ash trays, boxes, decanters) as well as just to look at (small pictures, drawings, porcelains, flowers, plants). They soften and mellow and pin point and sharpen, and document the youness of you. They have a way of looking only as good as they really are, though legerdemain in their arrangement can elevate second quality items to first. Exquisite taste in the choice and arrangement of accessories can be one of the interior designer's most cherished possessions, but of course only if he happens indeed to have it.

Conversation naturally goes around in circles, yet most conversational groupings or seating arrangements in rooms are set up along rectangular or parallel lines. Nothing encourages a sensibly circular conversational situation more than circular rugs on which seats gravitate into circles themselves. Large round rugs play beautifully against the squareness or rectangularity of a room; small ones against other small square or rectangular rugs. However if the round rug is to be the dominant design element in a room the colors and pattern should make it abundantly clear who's boss. Further, there should be an architectural or other separate visual reinforcement of the importance attached to the rug, like a circular molding on the ceiling directly over the rug. Almost all traditional types of rugs can be found in circular versions, except orientals. Yet I find myself making to order more of the round rugs I use than the rectangular; with **circular rugs** the exact size and exact design is somehow more important; maybe a round rug itself is more important just because it's round. Oval rugs count as circular rugs. And these rugs have distinguished third cousins in custom-shaped rugs which are straight on three sides and curved on one. But rounded rugs are pleasing only if their curves are compass-drawn arcs, not free form; a cloverleaf is more satisfactory than an amoeba. Much of the evil in mass-produced modern furniture flows from the free-form curve, which should be straightened out or curved right.

American eighteenth and nineteenth century furniture has been assigned the adjective "early" by the public, and I wish the public would disassign it, for eighteenth and nineteenth century American furniture is no earlier than French or English eighteenth and nineteenth century furniture. Most American furniture copied, more or less accurately, English models, but there was also some imitation of French. With the single exception of Jefferson—who was architect, curtain designer, fabric coordinator, color engineer, and ébéniste—no American president gave a hoot or holler about interior design, and the thought of sponsoring a national period in design, as the Kings Louis did, never entered their heads, though isolated new individual pieces like the Philadelphia highboy did turn up. Thus, if we except contemporary American design (which is a pyramid rising from a broad base of abominable, through gradually diminishing areas of acceptable, through still smaller areas of good, to a little point which is our truly excellent design) the only design complex native to America is Shaker—provincial furniture as pure and upright as the Quakers who began making it in the eighteenth century and still do, unchanged, today. Otherwise, most carefully made antique **100 american furniture** so resembles its European models, being ever so subtly heavier here or lighter there, that only an expert can assign it to this side of the Atlantic or that.

102 In bullish times the **decorative hardware** production curve always shoots up; when people are making money they find these little luxuries perversely appealing because they think they can so easily be done without. But you can't open most doors and drawers without some kind of at least functional hardware, and so it really makes sense to insist that it be decorative too. Not only the doorknob and the back rose from which it emerges, but hinges, nails, and screws can be decorative. But if you're going to the exercise to acquire a decorative doorknob you are better advised not to get a doorknob at all, but a lever handle—so much more practical to turn, and so much more attractive, being in greater relief and thinner; anything thinner is prettier. Small drawer or door pulls—boutons to the French—might better not be simple little "buttons" at all, but decorative diamonds, lozenges, ovals, stars, squares, flowers, or whatever. In our present era of admiration for entire walls devoted to built-in storage, such hardware is one of few devices that can interrupt the monotony and give distinction and variety to the clinical efficiency.

No other decorative device or object can accomplish so much per dollar as wallpaper. Expanses which would look empty if merely painted look furnished when papered. The old cliché about the size of the room's dictating the size of the pattern of the paper—delicate designs for small rooms, bold designs for large—should be ignored. The pattern of the paper should be selected not according to the size of the room but to what usually happens in it. Bold, brilliant, overscaled papers are not usually pleasant to relax with in rooms of any size. However, theatrical patterns can be superb in foyers, halls, dining rooms, bathrooms, and other rooms large or small in which people do not normally repose for extended periods. Jolts can be a joy, but only when you're supposed to be on your feet or sitting up straight anyway. Wallpaper by its very nature is imitative, but rare among the world's imitations because it often turns out more interesting than the marble, wood, scenic vistas, flowers, fabric, or architectural elements it imitates. Wallpaper, unlike paint, ought to be applied professionally. Patterns must be flawlessly matched. And paper really should be lined. The amateur always questions the extra effort and expense lining paper requires. But lined **104 wallpaper** stays up better and looks better. Even a casually practiced eye can usually tell at a glance whether or not a paper is lined, which precludes any further discussion.

The splendor and classical antecedents of French Empire appealed to the British who, during the period called **106 english regency**, imitated it all but intact. There was widespread enthusiasm for an exaggeration of Greek and Egyptian shapes, curves and objects, though a road or two led also to Rome. Doric and Ionic orders were standard components of furniture and architectural design. Klismos chair backs, honeysuckle, cornucopias, abundant rosewood and black lacquer, marble and bronze busts and statues of classical philosophers and heroes, and deep brown, dark olive green and rich red walls confronted you at every turn. Jazzed-up Regency occurred from time to time, as in the Brighton Pavilion, but most of it was opulently restrained, simple, severe, elegant, and masculine, if such a combination of modifiers isn't mutually exclusive. The same thing was going on at more or less the same time not only in France but in Germany (Biedermeier) and America (Duncan Phyfe) and chances are that a French Empire, Biedermeier, or Duncan Phyfe piece could be found to fit any description of an English Regency piece without changing a syllable. You have to see the piece to see the difference, and know it to see it.

A diversion of artists is to assemble a satisfying arrangement of objects and to record the deed in paint or drawing. The artist deals with still lifes only when he feels like it, but the interior designer has to do it all the time. Every setting has to be considered as a still life, or succession of still lifes, or still lifes within still lifes in addition to its other duties. The artist has another advantage: if the color of the jug in his arrangement doesn't suit him he can simply paint it a color that does, but a decorator has to go out and unearth it. Also, the artist's still life doesn't ever have to work, as the decorator's almost always does. Moving life must pass smoothly in and around and through the combination of furniture, objects, color, texture, and scale that create the still life. Naturally, **108** since **still lifes** are arrangements of several objects large or small, major or minor, in various juxtapositions with one another, the elimination of any element can throw the whole thing out of plumb. When a client balks at the price of one of the objects in a still life the whole painstaking thing often has to be junked. There may be a good substitute for anything including the Mona Lisa if you can find it, but you can't find it. The one excuse for using a functional piece in a nonfunctional manner—like a mirror placed so it's impossible to see anything in it or a chair that can't be gotten at to sit in—is when the object is serving as member of a legitimate still life.

Folding screens should have French fabric hinges so that each panel may be folded backward or forward as the exigency of the situation indicates. Screens look good used ornamentally, flattened against a wall like a big picture; architecturally, to balance a vertical element elsewhere in the room; and utilitarianly too, to hide necessary or unremovable ugliness. French bedrooms have them to prevent drafts. The ones I use most are covered with antiqued wallpaper, fabric, leather, or mirror, and I like to outline each panel with cording, braid, or antique nailheads, except for mirrored panels, properly framed in wood. Unavoidable modern conveniences, like television sets and toilets, are less objectionable if hidden **110** behind **screens** whenever space allows them to be.

Apparently the English thought more of their cabinetmakers than the French, for the French identified their decorative periods with political labels while the British labeled many of theirs with names of the cabinetmakers themselves. Most magnitudinous star in the English star system was **112 chippendale** who actually turned into three stars, grandfather and father and son, which shone for a century. The Chippendale output was as prolific as Bach's, Haydn's, and Mozart's combined. Papa Thomas produced a famous book in 1754 which was literally a comprehensive catalogue of acceptable design and which, like Shakespeare's plays, influenced everybody ever after. He himself had been influenced by a most eclectic combination of styles including classic, French, Gothic, and Chinese. Hence there is no one trade-marking Chippendale leg as there is for so many other periods because from the Chippendale potpourri poured every leg imaginable—from cabrioles to balls and claws to clusters of bamboo to straight square ones too—and the furniture they supported ranged from barococo-orgy to classical-calm. However difficult it therefore is to generalize, most pieces at least were big (many English manor houses dwarf the palaces and chateaux of the continent). Most were mahogany. Most used curves to good purpose because Chippendale was the undisputed English master of the curve. Chippendale's finest years were those he shared with Adam, who held him down a little. Most famous Chippendale creation was the camel-back sofa.

114 I'm fond of ceramic tile and quarried tile floors, but fonder by far of **terra cotta tile** floors. You can have terra cotta tiles baked to order, to any size or shape to make any design you wish, and as pink or red or brown as you like, though it makes sense to me, since it's terra cotta to begin with, to choose a deep, true terra cotta color. But terra cotta bakers are a reluctant lot, and you may have to exhaust a good deal of persuasion and patience before your tiles are delivered. Once down, terra cotta tiles should be kept waxed to produce and sustain a patina so lovely that I'm often successfully tempted not even to lay a small rug on top of it. Please do not ask me why, because I don't know, but ceramic, quarried and terra cotta tile floors should actually not have borders.

The two great cuisines of the world are French and Chinese, and for my money the two great traditions of interior design and decoration are too. However, pure unrelieved Chinese overwhelms the western mind and eye, as a visit to even the most exquisitely decorated Chinese restaurant will remind you. Too much is going on in too many places too simultaneously. But when individual Chinese shapes and objects are extracted from the melee of an entirely Chinese setting and introduced with restraint into a western room, it's another matter. Chinese vases, in particular, make exquisite lamps which look right in a western interior of any period because their shape, like that of the column or the obelisk or the egg, leaves nothing to be wished. The best ones are likely to be Chinese red or black—the particular black called, accurately, mirror black—and they can be found if you look hard, quite where no one knows. Few rooms fail to be improved by a Chinese screen or rug, or Chinese bowls or porcelains, though the ubiquitous grinning Chinese lions are ugly, probably because real lions neither grin nor live in China. Chinese objects were once so cheap and plentiful that they were used as ballast on trading ships returning from the East; hence, while not so cheap, **chinese** decorations are still relatively **117** plentiful despite the post-World War II American embargo on Chinese goods. The only "cocktail" tables which can be authentically antique are Chinese—or at least oriental— because nobody else ever made tables low enough to qualify.

I'm hardly Carrie Nation, but really the only reason to have a built-in bar at home is just to illustrate the fact that you can. Bars are more trouble than they're worth. It's usually just as efficient to bring in the drinking paraphernalia from a normal kitchen or existing service area, and, in my opinion, more gracious really to have everything out and available and hospitable on a lovely tray right at hand when and where drinking is taking place. (Some people euphemistically reluctant to face facts feel that one function of a bar is to hide the bottles, but hiding bottles while drinking makes no more sense than hiding the food at dinner, does it now.) Portable **118 bars** also have the distinct advantage of being portable—crop-up-able anywhere in the house people may take it into their heads to have a drink. And when drinking is done, portable bars on trays may be totally removed, and not remain imposingly or ostentatiously around as a kind of monument to or enshrinement of glut. However if a client is undissuadably hell-bent to have a bar, I say OK, put it in the family room if there is one and make it a really elaborate combination of bar, soda fountain, and short-order stand so that as much use may be gotten out of this superfluity by as many members of the family, and as often, as possible.

Poor terraces—and poor porches and balconies everywhere! Only basements and garrets receive shorter shrift as repositories of the cast off. A terrace should be considered as an additional room which requires—and sometimes deserves— more maintenance and care than any other. It must be a projection of the personality of the interior. If there's no natural ceiling one should be created of canvas or, if you like your rain to patter, of tôle, because ceilings make terraces look larger. Woven canvas, with the pattern through and through, looks pretty to any neighbors looking down on your terrace as well as to you looking up, but if you don't care about them, printed canvas serves nicely. There is a greater proportion of badly designed metal outdoor furniture than any other; the few good pieces are used far too often, but one has little choice. During the winter, terraces are still important because you still see them. The Vicenza-stone flower baskets should remain, the statuary, the fountain with the water drained, and whatever plants and trees not harmed by cold. It is lovely to watch terra cotta statuary and pots weather to the mellow crumbliness of classical ruins almost before your eyes, before they actually disintegrate. Metals which turn gray or green as they corrode also derive benefit from weathering. Trellises, **120** planted or plain, work hard to make **terraces** appealing. The British and Americans have a heavy hand with wood. Trellises to covet are in the French style, with laths no more than an inch and a half wide and half an inch thick, as lacy and light as they can possibly be without courting collapse.

Individualists of all types, from rugged to polished, are attracted by the idea of rooms totally custom designed, where every last stick is conceived and made expressly to order. The least that you know about such a room is that nobody else on earth has one quite like it. At no other time does the interior designer find himself with so much rope, or so much danger of hanging himself with it. The temptation with carte blanche is always to go too whole hog in one direction or another; the custom designed room will be only as effective as the designer's self-discipline on this his field day. The object, of course, is to make the room both as attractive and as useful as possible, theoretically more likely when starting from scratch, but actually so only if the designer really knows **122** what he is about. **custom designed rooms** may be traditional in style as well as contemporary. They can be reminiscent without being imitative. Exquisitely designed custom furniture with no historical roots has potential value as antiques of the future; all design began as custom design.

124 People who feel **chintz** is low end, who would even presume to apply the adjective "chintzy" in a derogatory manner, are simply insecure in their own tastes or antecedents. The judicious—even sometimes the abandoned—use of chintz implies no bungalowesque disrespect, can pay a high compliment to almost any room, and for each part of dignity it may take away it contributes two parts of gaiety or charm. Even riots of chintz dare be decorously incited—half a dozen different chintzes may splash across a single room (but only provided their patterns differ radically from one another). Chintz—toile to the French—is printed cotton, glazed or unglazed. When upholstering with chintz careful attention must be devoted to arranging things so that the dominant element in the repeat lands in the middle of defined areas like seats and backs. One of the most satisfactory uses for chintz is as slipcovers for all the upholstered pieces in a room, and as curtains too, all in the same chintz for a dramatic seasonal change. This way, an all-solid winter room can become an all-pattern summer room. Many people like to accent the design of chintz used for upholstery with quilting. This strengthens the chintz, but fattens it, and tends to make upholstered pieces look flatulent. Chintz is a family affair; some of the heart goes out of it in interiors inhabited by single people.

Few antique porcelain stoves remain because, being porcelain, they are subject to all the accidents porcelain is congenitally heir to plus the additional occupational hazard of sudden temperature fluctuations from very cold to very hot. Nevertheless—and even though you can't see the fire—it's cheating to have a porcelain (or any) stove that's not hooked up to operate, and also fraudulent simply never to put an operable stove in operation. If decorating is to have integrity, and it is, everything which was created to work should always be equipped to work and should, at least now and then, be made **126** in fact to work. If **porcelain stoves** are really important or romantic they deserve to appropriate a niche or platform better to set themselves off. Once we find ourselves far enough removed in time from any period, representatives of its characteristic design acquire legitimacy even when crude and rude. So even a cast-iron Franklin stove can today be admitted to situations many cuts above its original low rank.

128 The art of **trompe l'oeil** painting is serious and tongue-in-cheek at the same time. Trompe l'oeil painting doesn't actually set out to fool the eye as the expression would indicate, but instead sets out to pretend to fool the eye, with both artist and viewer in tacit agreement on the let's pretend. Trompe l'oeil has once again come into widespread use because suddenly, as in the Renaissance and the eighteenth century, and after a long moratorium, many capable artists have become fascinated by the art, admittedly for a price. Conceivably any subject which exists—God-made or man-made—is fair game for trompe l'oeil treatment: vistas, reflections, architectural elements, still lifes, trellises, and strapwork, to name just a few. Palladian trompe l'oeil even included people peeking into windows and around doors, like Charles Addams' grandmother. No rule exists about where trompe l'oeil may be applied, either. It can go on walls, ceilings, furniture, accessories, or anything else. Marbleizing is a form of trompe l'oeil. Originally, trompe l'oeil painting was sometimes an economy. Painting ornamentation on furniture to look like metal cost less than casting and chasing the actual metal. Today trompe l'oeil imitation often costs more than the imitated, though this is hardly germane to a discussion of its use.

Two of almost anything are better than one, provided one of it is better than none. Pairs of chairs, benches, lamps, tables, sofas, chandeliers or what you will make a somehow restful and reassuring point, and can add up to far more than the sum of their parts. Contemporary pairs can be turned out at will; far more rare the antique pair. Rapacious dealers over the years have often found it profitable to split and sell fine old pairs separately, each member for more than half the going price for two. Or tradespeople may simply feel that a bird sold is better than two on hand in the shop, and break the pair with no more emotion than they'd waste crushing an ant. Once parted, the twain hardly ever meet. Yet I bought a Directoire pedestal in Berlin once and found its undoubted original twin in Peoria, where it had wandered via Munich.

130 Avoid placing more than three or four **pairs** in a room, or they'll give you the uneasy sensation that you're seeing double. Among even numbers, the only really satisfactory ones are two (as in pairs) and four (as in legs). Odd numbers are absolutely always preferable to half a dozen, the worst even number. (I never even quite know what to do with the sixth flower in the florist's half dozen; often discard it in despair.)

Floor lamps are for three reasons: easy and practical transportability, height, and subtlety of illumination. Obviously they are efficiently moved around because you don't have to figure out something to put them on; unlike table lamps, they stand on their own foot. Floor lamps allow a source of light in a room to come from a height intermediate between that from table lamps and chandeliers, for variety, and floor lamps tend to illuminate more generally, and hence more subtly than table lamps, which are more likely used to dramatize or pin point a specific area. Moved from place to place floor lamps create new combinations of light and shadows in a room, and shadows to me are a crucial by-product of lighting and a decorating tool of enormous stature. I love shadows. I love rooms full of chiaroscuro, of plants carefully lit to fling black lace on the wall, and of any pretty objects which repeat themselves in entire or partial enlargement as shadows, and I hate lighting-engineer diffused and indirect and shadowless lighting, because in such a room I feel vacuum packed. Further, not just Peter Pan but everybody is reassured to cast shadows personally. No antique floor lamps exist except torchères, but fortunately, contemporary designers have turned out dozens of really lovely ones, unusual of them. Some find

132 it amusing to make **floor lamps** out of electrified antique fire-screen poles because what was originally intended as a shield from light becomes a source of it, a pleasant reversal.

134 After just five minutes in the hush of the famous French silk **fringe and tassel** factory at Lyons, watching flying fingers wrap and tie with silk the myriad component tassels in every tassel, I resolved never again to complain that tasseled fringe runs up to $100 the yard and tassel and cord curtain tiebacks to $200 the pair, and, true to my resolution, have not.

136 Electrical **cords and plugs**, entirely unwelcome contemporary intrusions, have lower estate even than children, for they may not even be seen. The ideal way to conceal a cord is of course to build it right into the wall and permit it to emerge only at that point nearest the lamp or other apparatus it must supply. In lieu of architectural concealment any number of makeshift but effective camouflages may and should be arranged, depending upon the particular circumstances, the most obvious being to route a cord under a rug, or behind a piece of furniture or, if a table is involved, to let it run down its leg, tied to the back. Exposed so-called floor plugs, which as it turns out should more accurately be called wall plugs, are one of the curses of contemporary construction. Why builders do not use their heads and mount them inconspicuously smack at the floor in baseboards instead of in the wall a foot above is as incomprehensible as the plunging of the Gadarene swine into the sea. I feel it's important enough to have plugs in baseboards to move them there whenever I'm allowed, though it does eat into budget. A friend has an exposed cord that's permissible because it runs from lamp to floor through the mouth of an original Barye bronze lion, who seems to be running along with it like a poodle with a packet from a shop in its mouth, before passing on to a plug concealed behind a sofa. But I can't think of a single other exposed cord that I wouldn't hide if I could.

I like collections but I loathe the word. Somehow collecting is something you do to the rent or the garbage. Collections can either be massed together in a unified display, behind a velvet rope as it were, or dispersed through the house in a more subtle treatment which allows you always to be coming unexpectedly upon an obelisk or a piece of Creil or an article of Empire steel, each time with the fun of discovering an Easter egg. One of my own passions is eagles, of the rarer unferocious type which happens to appear on the seal of the President of the United States and also on my family crest. Eagles in predatory attitudes are a dime a dozen; in the greater challenge of finding good benign ones, in brass, carved wood, gilt, marble, glass, and so on, lies as much diversion as possessing them. Collecting becomes less of a fetish if the collection has some practical purpose. Guns can be shot, rare books can be read, tôle lamps can be seen by, which lifts

them above purely ornamental or compulsive **collections**. One of the most satisfactory useful things to collect is porcelain in the form of after-dinner cups and saucers of different designs, shapes, colors, and patterns. After dinner everyone can have his coffee in a different cup, giving him something interesting to look at and think, if not actually to talk, about.

Wall-to-wall carpeting has had its ups and downs in the prestige department over the years, sometimes representing the epitomization of high class and other times that of low. This has nothing to do with wall-to-wall carpeting generically, though, with which a person has the right to carpet any room in his house he feels like at any time, from foyer to bathroom, except the kitchen. Wall-to-wall stays the same no matter what fickle fashion thinks of it, rarely the best or the worst treatment to give a floor, often good to tie a disconnected room together, and always at least the easiest to maintain. Many people like it especially in bedrooms because for them it imparts quiet, warmth, and security conducive to a restful atmosphere. But there's a catch. For as it arrives at the walls, **140** **wall-to-wall** carpeting usually must be finished with some kind of woven-in border treatment to look right, and to be honest this in effect metamorphoses wall-to-wall carpeting into a rug. One way therefore to achieve wall-to-wall carpeting is to kill two birds at a stroke and find and lay an existing bordered rug that's the exact size of a room. Oddly shaped small rooms or large rooms of any shape must receive custom wall-to-wall treatment though, and if the (expensive) specially-woven border must be omitted, the efficacy of a wall-to-wall treatment in the first place should be re-examined to be sure that, borderless, the carpet will not look naked. I bet it will.

142 ormolu—brass or bronze doré applied decoration—began dressing up French furniture during the baroque period. Usually it was most comfortable on city furniture inclining toward elegance, but guileless provincial pieces often found themselves being decked out in a set of ormolu if they moved to town. Besides being simply ornamental these various molded motifs sometimes serve structural purposes, helping to brace the furniture, or, in the case of sabots, to provide its feet and actually hold it up, and sometimes incorporate themselves into the fundamental design, as when ormolu is made to fit into the fluting of a Louis XVI leg. The various periods of design of course dictated the design of ormolu produced during them, and if you want to nit pick as I do not, I suppose it is improper to fasten ormolu of one period onto furniture of another. Other decorations akin to ormolu applied to backs of chairs and to the aprons and sides of other furniture are Wedgwood placques, and inserts of tôle, mirror, eglominse, and marble. Hitchcock naïvely, and though often charmingly, imitated ormolu with gold paint and stencils in America.

Bogus or suspect antique "originals" are less valuable and less to be desired than faithful reproductions of the real thing. What a blessing that accurate reproductions are entirely socially acceptable; even if we wanted to we couldn't put genuine antiques into every room of every house because there obviously aren't that many antiques. While I'm certainly not pro-reproduction and anti-antique I do think too much fuss that really doesn't matter a jot is made over antiques; for example, all of the energy expended on extolling the virtues of signed pieces might better be applied elsewhere, for nobody knows whose signatures most of the signatures on signed pieces were. If a piece a hundred or more years old isn't of the period—made during the time and in the country that such original furniture was being made—it isn't an antique at all, but an antique reproduction. But unless a reproduction is faithful it automatically becomes an original itself, and 99 and 44/100ths per cent of the time a bastard one. Don't knock Grand Rapids which is as capable of producing satis-

144 factory **reproductions** as monstrous ones. The wood in domestic furniture is attuned to our climate and less subject to the warpings, splittings, and other internal upheavals that some contemporary imported furniture seems to fall victim to.

Guess why parquet floors in virtually all post-World War II buildings aren't quite kosher parquet—they don't have a border, without which true parquet is impossible. Otherwise **146 wood floors** are either parquet or not, depending upon whether boards are laid in a pattern (squares or herringbones or other geometric designs or designs within designs) or simply in parallel rows. Proper parquet connotes a certain distinction, but no one need burst with anything but pride when putting the snootiest, most regal antiques on a floor of rustic parallel boards of various widths, held down or together with pegs or butterfly wedges, beautifully stained and waxed. A joy of either floor lies in the different effect staining has on different individual boards and their graining. Importantly or exquisitely parqueted floors should not be stained too dark or the design will be lost. Indifferently parqueted ones and parallel board ones offer their owners a choice: either to stain them fairly dark and keep the play of graining against graining, or to stain them very dark, lose the graining, and gain the greater elegance (and heart-and-headaches) really dark wood floors deliver on a polished platter. With floors of parallel boards all the same width the choice is withdrawn. They must be stained very dark, and become no longer ugly.

More attention is popularly given to what's going to happen to table tops than to the table tops themselves, and of course the answer to what's going to happen to them is absolutely everything. No matter what material they're made of, no matter what protestations of virtue and faith you receive from makers of tops or finishes or preservatives or preventatives, they're going to be stained or broken or scratched or burned or torn or cut or disfigured in some way, and maybe all. Plate and Carrara glass can't be stained but can be scratched and smashed. Marble can be scratched and smashed and stained for good measure. Waxed wood, lacquer, upholstery, and leather are prey to even wider ranges of disasters. My personal advice about how to cope with the inevitable is to relax and enjoy it, and to live with table tops you like regardless of how impractical you think them because more practical ones that you didn't like would turn out to be impractical too. Some people impose a limit of two marble tops to a room, but they are old wives full of tales; go ahead

148 and make all the **table tops** in a room marble if you want to, especially if there's a lot of wood around elsewhere. Plate-glass tops include the design of the table base—and the rug—in the table top design because, of course, you can see through them. On bureaux plats where leather tops are desired the leather should match the color of the wood or finish of the base as much as possible. Otherwise you'll spend all your time looking at the leather top instead of the base.

Some of my clients, urged to do so by me, possess several different sets of slipcovers in order to enjoy an almost complete change of mood several times a year. In all cases the **slipcovers** are made with as much care and skill and attention to detail and fit as the upholstery they slipcover. Trimmings should be in the upholstery league too: seams require braid or fringe if not piped or welted. Skirts must be flat, may be scalloped or shaped at the bottom, and may have pleats at corners only. No one may have pleats anywhere else, and only very young and silly ladies are allowed ruffles, which, when they grow up, must come off. Seating upholstered in light-colored fabrics should have permanent slipcovers in the identical fabric. These slipcovers are in place all the time except when being cleaned. By scheduling cleanings for periods of minimum traffic, the actual upholstery is likely to come through unscathed for years and the eye of the owner is never offended by a disrupted everything's-out-for-spring-renovation look because the furniture looks the same whether the slipcovers are on or off. Slipcovers should be made of tightly woven fabric to protect upholstery beneath from dust.

The art form known as the ash tray has evolved in our own century, with much more attention to function than to form, as a glance into the windows of any gift or crystal shop will instantly confirm. Because there are so few pretty ash trays made for the purpose, virtually any setting requires a scattering of porcelain, glass, or pottery saucers. But saucers used as ash trays should never be nor look like contemporary saucers. An indentation in the saucer for the base of the cup may not occur. Many unindented saucers exist, because this is the way the French and Viennese made them for coffee or chocolate cups. They are also smaller than conventional **152 saucers** manufactured today, and have high sides, either straight or curved, the more effectively to contain the ashes. When companion cups have survived intact, they make excellent (and perforce matching) repositories for cigarettes. Naturally the color of the saucers, and cups if any, should relate to the general scheme. Many are hand painted, many old ones are frankly works of art, every bit as first class to have around as fine vases or figurines of the same material. People with passion for dishes can incidentally indulge themselves with saucer ash trays instead of hanging plates on the wall, a barbarism. There is nothing extravagant about using fine porcelain for ashes—good things should always be in use. And the better the porcelain the less likely it is to be stained by cigarette tars; avoid porcelain cracked through the glaze.

One of our American tragedies is that the vast majority of our rooms suffer from lack of height, and that the oppressive low altitude of most ceilings is made oppressively lower—the ceiling is pulled down nearer to zero—through misguided use of horizontal elements everywhere: sofas, tables, pictures. True, you can't ever have a very vertical sofa, but ceilings should **154** at least be pushed up with **vertical pictures**, which can push very hard indeed. Far fewer vertical than horizontal pictures exist, of course; too bad that most artists feel compelled to operate horizontally because most of the time their subjects could have been as successfully composed vertically. At any rate, in lieu of vertical pictures, two or more horizontal ones can be hung above and below one another to give an overall vertical impression—often enhanced by hanging the narrower picture(s) at the bottom, producing an inverted pyramid of satisfying El Greco-like instability. A great vogue holds sway for grouping a swarm of pictures together on a wall, sometimes obliterating it entirely, like a plague of locusts. This makes it impossible for the eye to pull any one picture out of the general visual cacophony, and reduces pictures to the merely supporting role of wallpaper; extravagant.

Large plants are full of theater. They are invaluable in disguising architectural caprices. If there are a number of plants, the shapes of the leaves and the shades of green should contrast. Masses of plants can be attractive, but each must repose in an interesting jardiniere (simple wood ones assorted among more elegant brass, bronze, and ceramic ones), and an excessively hack-through-it-with-a-machete look is wise to avoid however green one's thumb or billfold. Plants are an economy when compared to flowers. They accomplish more spacially and, with care, last indefinitely even shut up in town; a friend of mine whose plants never die says it's because he keeps a night crawler in each to tend to cultivation. Haphazard arrangements are better in contemporary settings, geometrically precise ones in formal. Plants can hide unsightly views when placed in front of windows you don't care to look out of, yet because they are a function of the outdoors they convey the idea of windowness, even when windows are viewless. Tall vertical plants, like vertical pictures, help push up the ceiling. Dripping or flowing ones look cottage if not downright dimestorey. Pleasant groupings of plants with sculpture are easy to bring off. Stark settings virtually require **156 plants** for softening. Creative placement of lamps can also create fascinating and softening shadows and silhouettes. Artificial plants are invited into any setting provided that they look either so real—or so artificial—as to forestall any conjecture.

No more unjustly neglected decorative objects can be found than fountains, hard to find in American interiors indeed. Yet they are as appropriate, if not actually more so, indoors as out; in the same league as fireplaces, they provide a fine point of interest; and because of the rotary pump, plumbing is not required and fountains may be positioned according to whim. **158** Freestanding pedestal **fountains** do more work of furnishing than wall fountains. Some attention should be directed when shopping for a fountain to the visible or apparent source of water. When water emanates from the mouths or other anatomical apertures of boys, maidens, fish, or animals an encroachment upon good taste rarely fails to occur. Water more satisfactorily flows or spurts or splashes forth from inanimate sources, say, a vase held under the arm of a nymph. Fountains are not just to look at but to hear—unlike loudly ticking or chiming clocks, the sound of the water is unobtrusive and restful, true even with passionate fountains like those at Tivoli, and the sound may be varied beyond its natural endless variations by regulating the speed of the pump. Lead and marble fountains tend to be more formal than wood, stone, and cement fountains, but no one really cares about this.

160 animal skins are the oldest kind of floor covering. When flinging a skin on the floor became no longer a matter of simple expediency, the practice was perpetuated by hunters who wished to walk about on proof of their prowess. Only recently have skins fallen into fashion for purely aesthetic reasons—high time, because nothing is more frankly Sybaritic than the look of a leopard, jaguar, or tiger against a highly polished dark floor. Skins should retain the shape of the animal with neck, tail, and paws defined, unless several skins are matched and stitched into a larger rectangular rug. Stuffing and retaining the heads of the animals themselves is discouraged. Heads invariably look either fierce or pathetic and besides, when they are three dimensional you trip over them. They also preoccupy attention from the beauty of the fur and further, if the hunter was a good one, he shot the animal in the head to avoid mutilating the body, and few taxidermists qualify as plastic surgeons. The traditional way to finish skins is with an underlining of scalloped felt or flannel —it may be black, brown, or billiard table green—which extends a few inches beyond the animal as a border. Lions and bears can best be avoided, but low-pile animals which perform pleasantly as floor coverings are zebras, ponies, and thoroughbred cows. Spotted Guernseys and Holsteins are fine, though I prefer Jerseys of a more delicate than usual fawn.

Mirroring turns a niche into a shadow box or, more accurately, a reflecting box. In the interest of more pleasantly complicated reflections I like to include two mirror panels in addition to those for the two sides and back, making the mirror 5/8ths of an octagon and less like a miniature barbershop. Such a niche has a practical as well as decorative purpose, for it permits objects displayed in the niche to be seen in the round, worthwhile, of course, only if the backs of such objects are attractive. The top and bottom of the niche should be mirrored too to pick up and repeat all the reflections possible. Cylindrical niches can't very well be mirrored with a round concave mirror, and would look like a fun house if they could. Each of the mirror inserts must be planes, really, and you may decide that the unreflecting roundness of your cylindrical niche pleases you more than a reflecting 5/8ths octagon would. Yet, you'll find so few other people with **162** **mirrored niches** that it would be nice to go ahead and mirror a cylindrical niche anyway if you have one around.

The two great rugs of France are Savonnerie and Aubusson. The Savonnerie is a pile chenille (which fewer people than you'd think know is the French word for caterpillar). The Aubusson evolved as a flat, coarse tapestry weave, with individual color elements woven as separate entities and then fitted into place like pieces of a jigsaw puzzle and stitched fast with silk. Natural enemies of the Aubusson are ladies' high heels and needlelike furniture legs; even with a stout lining (the stoutest has overlapping circles of lining material appliquéd onto the lining proper for good measure) the rugs are fragile as frosting, accidents occur, repairs are frequent. The softness of the Savonnerie chenille might suggest more luxury to some, but I prefer Aubussons and think them prettier partly because the design is so precisely defined and never blurred by pile rising and falling and melting together. The Bessarabian rug, also woven in a tapestry weave, is brother if not father to the Aubusson, but reversible and unlined, unlike the Aubusson which can't be turned over because it has a right and wrong side, with a welter of threads running at cross purposes on the wrong, and must be lined for aesthetic as well as utilitarian purposes. Since the original Moors came from Spain and established the first rug looms in the town of Aubusson in the middle ages, designs of the rugs have constantly changed as they reflected the preferences of each period. Miro, Picasso, Braque, Cocteau, and other contemporary artists have produced cartoons from which Aubussons are being woven in **aubusson** today, and so have I.

Eyes always fly straight up to the ceiling as they enter any room, perhaps because light, like heat, goes up. So it's nice to give them something to look at when they get there, like **166 decorated ceilings**. Ceiling decoration may range from elaborate (the Sistine Chapel) to simple (a marbleized or glazed panel from which a chandelier may sprout). Painted skies in dining rooms and foyers give a welcome illusion of openness and height. Painted or real trellises and strapwork which create the illusion of even greater height beyond give height too. (With today's printed acoustical tile you can put up an architectural ceiling and wall treatment that has a printed trellis effect.) But whatever you do you'll make the same discovery that Michelangelo did—that doing anything on a ceiling is harder because a ceiling's always up there and never down here—and lesser ceiling ornamenters than Michelangelo are also likely to have a wicked time with perspectives. The least expensive way to decorate a ceiling probably is to wallpaper, and the most expensive in established use is to work with cast and molded plaster. A ceiling vaulted in segments decorates itself with pretty flowings of light and shade. But you can't decorate a ceiling with anything but an overall pattern unless it is a properly prescribed area, free of odd beams, projections, intrusions, or eccentricities. Otherwise the decoration simply emphasizes a misdemeanor better ignored.

Maybe because there's so much of it locked up in Fort Knox, gold has the reputation of being a more pretentious decorating device than silver. It is not. In fact, with its mellow warmth, **gold and gilt** can be a lot friendlier and more hospita-

ble than silver, which after all has the exact cold hard color of steel. Vermeil—gold-plated sterling silver—has never been turned out in great profusion partly because of its expense but mostly because we are so conditioned to silver for table service that the very word for table service is silver. Again no more pretentious than silver, vermeil can even be mixed with silver at the same table without insulting the former or upstaging the latter. Gold leaf on furniture and picture frames also contributes warmth rather than pretentiousness unless one has gold leafed the entire inventory. One leafing process —not dissimilar to that used in glazing a wall—calls for applying a coat of white gesso to a raw wood furniture frame, then a coat of color any color, then a layer of gold leaf (always applied with a flat brush called a gilder's tip which must be sable) rubbed so that some of the color beneath shows through, and results in a lush, unvulgar effect. Gold leaf applied to raw metal, then rubbed so that some of the metal color shows through, and lacquered creates a look of sophis-ticated texture for a contemporary table. I never use gold paint, nor should anyone, but always leaf, plate or solid gold.

High-back chairs, a refreshing change of pace in settings where other seating all rises to about the same thirty-inch back height, serve a function similar to stools and benches, but in an opposite way. They relieve just plain chairness by overstating instead of understating. Unless they happen to be **170** fat or ungainly specimens **high-back chairs** give high vertical return on low floorspace investment. For this reason they make good quotation marks to set off consoles in narrower, more heavily navigated areas like hallways. They don't have to be against a wall, but they should be placed where it isn't necessary to move them because even when they aren't physically heavy the act of moving them is usually unattractive to see even a footman perform. See-through ones give you verticality with the added bonus of not blocking vision. No rocking chairs, please, high-back or low; I have never seen a pretty one, I've looked, so I conclude that there is none. And anyway what an unpleasant distraction to watch somebody else rocking. It can't happen if there's no rocker.

Here is a catalogue of evils one or more of which most **172 fireplace-chimneypieces** are made to endure, perpetrations bad enough in themselves but compounded as the fire inevitably gathers the principal seating group close around it, where inspection can be leisurely and minute: Using white birch logs which jump out at you from the blackness. Permitting the absence of a desirable over-all burned-in look; interior walls of new fireplaces should be painted soot-black throughout. Suffering andirons to be out of scale with the chimneypiece, particularly in regard to height, and also to differ in period; unions of andirons and mantels may not be mixed. Indulging in the use of house bricks to construct the fireplace proper; the only permissible fireplace bricks are brickettes. Keeping fire screens, most of them ugly though I have one that isn't, in sight when not actually in use. Condoning any lack of harmony between period of chimneypiece and the totality of other periods represented in the setting. Clogging pretty, carved wood chimneypieces with paint instead of simply leaving them waxed and unclogged. Placing a white marble chimneypiece against a white wall. Failing to glaze stone mantels the color of the walls, especially if the walls are glazed. And, last and worst, displaying family photographs or flowing plants on the mantel. Electric bulb "fires" are beneath mention. So are fake fireplace-chimneypieces. Since you can see at a glance that they don't and can't have depth for the "fire," they get caught in their lie, *inflagrante delicto.*

Though not as gauche as the world thinks, America seems at least too indelicate in any of its climates to produce mulberry trees to suit the palate of the producing silkworm. Thus we have no domestic silk, and must get it all from Europe, manufacturer of silk since the ninth century, and the orient. Silk goes anywhere from pillows to parachutes, knows as many roles as any operatic diva worth her claque, may appear as velvet, taffeta, faille, moire, matelassé, brocatelle, lampas, brocade, to name just a few. Most elegant, maybe, is damask, with its design emerging as woven interplay between shiny and matte finishes. In strength, silk beats all other natural fibers, though not unnatural ones like nylon. Silk has a propensity for dyeing and for fading: just as well the F.T.C. won't let people guarantee silk won't fade because it will. Linen is the oldest known fiber. But silk, the most upper crust, discovered by the Chinese (who discovered so much beauty for the world of decoration) a couple thousands years B.C., is no chicken. If you're on the gold standard you use silk. Except for **174** furniture, my single biggest bill in business is my **silk** bill.

Bathrooms more often than any other room are allowed to go to hell in a handbasket, and this is sad because so much time is spent in them. While the bathroom may be a functional mayhem in the A.M., at other times it serves as auxiliary beauty parlor, recital hall, playroom, spa, and library, and as such should be handled with more care. Unless the bathroom has Romanesque proportions, and then only if your liability coverage is high, the tub should not be sunken. Unless in a fraternity house, humorous or risqué drawings, slogans or gimmicks should not be allowed to gravitate to the bath as they surely will if not actively prohibited. Unless it is the scene of frequent naval battles, the ubiquitous tile dado running around the walls makes no sense, as it does for tub and

shower walls. Because most **bathrooms** are so small and chopped up, anything which unifies is good. Walls and ceilings can be drawn into one by papering with wallpaper treated against moisture. The floor should be tied into the scheme with wall-to-wall carpeting or vinyl tile unless the original floor is tiling or marble of an acceptable design, as it never is. Tubs are a space-hogging superfluity if the user of the bath takes showers only. Rapport should exist between the bathroom and the bedroom you enter it from. Gold fixtures are no more grand than chrome or silver ones. Requiring little care, gold is in fact more practical (if the maid avoids abrasives).

178 Successful contemporary settings are rarely undiluted contemporary. The **contemporary** lump usually must be leavened by traditional elements or accents; otherwise the *gestalt* can all too easily turn out to be high showroom. Taken straight, the starkness and boldness of contemporary design is often simply too inhospitable and institutional and undistinguished to live in, and should be broken up and softened. Therefore, my contemporary settings tend to be tempered ones, with beautiful objects from a variety of past periods mellowing and modifying the present tense. An antique steel, Louis XVI, Directoire, Biedermeier, or a classical Chinese piece can give character and the warmth of years to a room while by no means encroaching upon its contemporaneousness. Reception areas of beauty parlors or fur salons may be "modern," but a room to live in must be either contemporary or traditional which, if contemporary, means both.

Just as the Louis XV period might more accurately be called the Madame Pompadour period and the Louis XVI the Marie Antoinette, the Empire period should rightfully be called the Napoleon. For, unlike the Kings Louis, Napoleon himself was the catalyst deliberately and purposefully responsible for the new look of the furnishings of his period. With a man instead of a woman behind the man with the chisel, pegs, and glue, one might expect **empire** furniture to be more masculine in concept than its predecessors. And sure enough, the new look was as revolutionary as Dior's. Napoleon's aim was to point up the obsolescence of the monarchy everywhere. His goal was to make everything as unlike what had been done for the kings, yet elegant and extravagant, as possible; he succeeded, even to the point of managing to spend more money, no incidental trick. Probably because Napoleon fancied himself a cross between Ramses II, Achilles, and Caesar, Empire took inspiration from classical Egypt, Greece, and Rome, with X's, columns with capitals and bases, pediments, severe lines, obelisks, sphinxes, and classically draped figures all over the place. Scale and silhouette were sumptuous and splendid. Colors were frank and forthright. Anybody who made anything that could be stuck on anything—ormolu, moldings, gimp, galloon, and trimmings—flourished like the green bay tree. And not even the green bay tree flourished like the mahogany tree—the imperial wood of the empire.

182 Good **drawings**, always better than bad or indifferent paintings, have an appeal of their own not the least of which is their comparative low cost—chic at half the price. People who can't afford to splash their walls with paintings of the masters turn to drawings because they are more subtle and understated, and so overlooked in the market place. Because drawings tend to be smaller than paintings, clustering them in bunches is OK, but an entire wall should never be plastered with them. Delicate as they usually are, drawings usually require thin frames—but making a small drawing larger and more important by matting it with a wide mat is legitimate. Those who know enough to care prefer so-called French mats, with molded, pressed, or embossed concentric rectangular borders, one or more of which may be ornamented with gold or silver paper. If the drawing has color, purists often prepare an identically matching wash with which to tint the mat. Be careful of nonreflecting glass, for it often adds an undesirable color cast of its own to the (delicate) drawing underneath. More often than not the virtues of the more expensive nonreflecting glass lie principally in the eye of the framer whose other eye lies principally in the till. In most locations in most rooms it turns out there's little for ordinary glass to reflect.

If an upholstered chair or sofa has an exposed wooden frame, the demarcation line between fabric and wood must be acknowledged in one of three ways. This may be done with ornamental nailheads. Or with single welting. Or with gimp. All three of these methods of finishing upholstery are purely ornamental, since the actual work of pulling the fabric tight to the frame is done by concealed upholstery tacks. Yet only an amateur, or an indifferently trained professional, could be so remiss as to allow one of the three not to occur. My own preference runs to gimp, because of the literally endless designs, weaves, fibers, textures, and colors that gimp comes in. Gimp may be used to play up or play down the meeting of fabric and wood, can quietly "finish" the fabric or punctuate it with an exclamation point. Gimp never turns a sow's ear into a silk purse. But it makes clear that a silk purse is indeed silk. Gimp in common use runs as high as $10 a yard —a lot the frugal may think for skinny braid. But because a few feet can do so so much it is unwise to skimp on **gimp**.

Far more important than the kind or pattern of wood in a wood floor: the color of the wood. The single most heinous decorative abomination is a yellow wood floor, perfectly hideous in itself, and a malignant quicksand which instantly engulfs anything you may put into the room and, for good measure, the whole room. If you move into a new apartment building with yellow floors which a perverse management forbids you to stain, immediately stain them. Whatever price you must pay for "restoring" them when you leave—from scraping them to tearing them up and replacing them—is smaller than even twenty minutes of life on yellow floors. Wood floors should, unless there is a good reason to the contrary of which I can think of none, be stained and waxed dark, and the darker—the blacker—the better, up to and including absolutely black patent. You get floors this way by using black walnut stain—not stain that you get from the black walnut tree, but dark walnut stain laced liberally with lampblack. You keep them this way with wax laced with same. Categorically, the most elegant floor of any kind in existence is the mirror polished jet-black wood floor. But slaves must be all but dis-emancipated to keep floors this way, for they show every fleck of dust and slipper scuff; you can see where a pin dropped. The wise owner or warden of such a floor adopts the Japanese custom of requiring everyone to remove his street shoes and substitute the softest slippers (which may still do some damage) at the door. Never any dancing except the gentlest waltzing in well-stockinged feet on **black wood floors**. **187**

Trying to establish a watertight distinction between gimp and galloon could reduce strong men to tears. Both are braids and both are trimmings; gimp is always made expressly to finish upholstery, but galloon can be used on upholstery too, as well as on curtains, draperies, pillows, lampshades, and fabric walls. Generally speaking, gimps are always narrower and galloons are always wider, though conceivably an unusually narrow **188** example of **galloon** could be narrower than an unusually wide example of gimp. Trimmings pull far more than their share of the load in any room. For these are what make a room personal and individual and unlike any other. By coincidence a friend or neighbor might have the same chair or sofa or draperies you have, but the odds are a trillion to one against her designer's having chosen the same trimmings. While I never deliberately set out to devote a definite portion of the budget to trimmings, it is not uncommon to estimate ten per cent of the money available for an entire job in this way. This news sometimes visibly curls the hair of clients seeking professional assistance for the first time. Mercifully, reservations melt away when clients can see, after the fact, that the finishedness of the finished job could not occur without gimp, fringe, and/or galloon. There are also apt to be alarums & excursions if a client happens to notice that a given trimming cost more than the total bill for the drapery fabric being trimmed. Yet this also may often prudently have been the case.

Almost as much of a logistical nuisance as wastebaskets and ash trays, which must be emptied directly after use, are flowers, which must be removed upon approaching death, always imminent, their life being as uninsurable as that of a Puccini heroine at curtain time. Far less demanding and in **190** the long run far more economical, **unreal flowers** can be as attractive, though not in the same way, as real ones. For me they're at their best when patently unreal—made of porcelain, glass, fabric, wood, metal, stone. Plastic ones produced to date, with their embalmed oily-transparent look, should be led away and shot, and beaded ones, created by the Italians for graves, painfully destroyed. Straw flowers have the knack of living and dying well, preserve themselves in death as attractively as the ancient Egyptians did, and bloom on as real flowers—with unobjectionably artificial overtones.

Tastefully upholstered headboards are both luxurious and a pain in the neck to keep that way, because headboards of beds are congenitally accident prone. Therefore I do my best to insist that an upholstered headboard have a matching slip-cover affair of the same material and design so that the headboard underneath, often quite literally a board, is never left exposed during cleanings or washings. Besides dressing up a bed headboards make beds appear more comfortable, though of course since you don't sleep on the headboard, this can be but an illusion. The fabric covering the headboard and the bed itself must be identical, and curtains surrounding the bed should be, and those at the windows of the bedroom can be, too. I often apply braid in scrolls to a headboard upholstered in plain fabric and repeat the same braid on the bedspread in a large rectangle slightly smaller than the surface of the bed itself to make the bed look less clumsy, as beds

192 tend to look. **upholstered headboards** may be outlined in wood, but I never use carved or intricately designed wood because the bedroom is the dustiest room in the house, and carvings defy dusting. Tufted headboards do too. And when tufted, they convey the suggestion that the principal function of the room is other than innocently to sleep in.

194 There's no more luxurious or worthwhile way to waste space than to devote it to a foyer or gallery or entrance hall far larger than the size of the rest of the house or apartment apparently deserves. Large **galleries** in small houses keep the secret of the smallness of the house as safe as a numbered account in a Swiss bank. They welcome the guest, impress him, and speed him graciously into the intimacy (or grandeur) beyond. You're allowed to pull out all the dramatic stops in entrance areas since no one properly enters or leaves for very long, and even the overpowering doesn't have enough chance to overcome. Wall and ceiling treatments merit special attention because usually there is little furniture. Contrary to popular belief, what furniture there is must be superb at all costs because the entrance hall establishes the mood of the rest of the place and, through its brief but effective conditioning, subliminally encourages even the observant to overlook minor omissions or lapses in the rooms within. One essential is a large mirror for entering guests to see how they withstood the trip to the house and, when departing, with what success their appearance survived whatever adventures befell them there.

Details which are sins of omission can be bad enough—for want of a nail the shoe was lost, etc., and for want of a finger **196** the dike would have failed. But **details** which are sins of commission are worse. I carry my passion for detail to the point of using only white pencils at the office so if I happen to lay one down on a swatch of fabric being presented to a client there can be no perhaps disastrous color clash. An opulent gold bathroom can be jarred to its plumbing by a single pink toothbrush exposed to view, or an antagonistically colored soap. Facial-tissue boxes, matchboxes, cigarette packages— in fact any commercial container, especially those advertised to be in decorator colors—should be destroyed, hidden away, or masked in special containers or slipcovers. All advertising should be banished; no container should be exposed to view anywhere, even in kitchens or dressing rooms, unless attractive. Restaurant matchbooks are name droppy to leave around if the restaurant is elegant or in another country, demeaning if it is not. It is unnecessary to remind people that they are in your house by monogramming guest towels, or that they have been there by leaving "personalized" matches about for them to pocket and take off. Flowers, even when sent in advance (hopefully never brought) by a guest may not appear when their color quarrels; ignorance is no excuse: if this is the guest's first visit he should surely have sent white. A hostess should naturally dress in harmony with her *locus operandi.*

Whether driven by masochism or the law of inconspicuous consumption or simply in an attempt to keep warm without central heating, our ancestors, when they papered a wall, papered a wall—first with cotton, burlap, or canvas, then with plain paper, and only then with decorative paper. So doing, they unwittingly played into our hands, for paper thus mounted may often be removed relatively intact and re-used today. Many such antique wallpapers, attractive to begin with, have become even more appealing as fading accomplished what no artist or fresh-mixed colors could. Any paper produced prior to 1830 may be considered antique. There were scenics and panels and patterns too. All were either painted by hand or printed with wooden blocks, one for each color, corresponding to silk screens today but with charming irregularities in registration, and because making paper in continuous rolls hadn't occurred to anybody yet, small individual sheets were simply pasted together. Luck is with you if you can find enough of an antique paper to do an entire room, not to mention pay for it. Bits and pieces of **antique wallpapers** are more common—enough to line a niche or cover a screen or, if really fragmentary, to be framed and hung as pictures.

198

Doors are one of those rare phenomena in interior decoration which should usually be made either quite inconspicuous or quite conspicuous and hardly ever left as is somewhere in between. Often the course of inconspicuousness is the more intelligent to take. If a flat, plain door tends to melt into a wall anyway, or to lead to an unglamorous place like a broom closet, or to be one of too many doors, it can be more easily ignored if wallpapered or painted exactly as the walls and adorned with minimal hardware. However if the door is one you simply cannot miss, or if it has real beauty of its own, it should have a fuss made over it and be staged like a prima donna. One way to play up doors is through use of overdoors, such as carved wood or painted panels or other decoration which call attention to the door and incidentally accent its valuable verticality. Doors may be framed with paint or architecture. Moldings and panels can be applied to the doors themselves, with greater drama if contrasting sharply in color against the body of the door. Doors can be upholstered in fabric or leather, or covered with mirrored panels. Fabric or open trelliswork panels can be built right in. French doors, of framed if not paned glass, are self-ornamental. Elegant hardware for doors is available in limitless selection, and leaves no excuse for ordinary doorknobs on important doors.

200 Decorative **doors** which fold back upon themselves are the logical means to close off from time to time an area like a dining room which you want not closed off most of the time.

The importance of the chandelier in a room automatically establishes the importance of the total decoration. To hang a chandelier that's underscaled for the situation is to commit another deadly decorating sin. In dining rooms the lowest part of the chandelier, which must be scaled for the table or vice versa, can hang no more (or less) than thirty-seven inches above the top of the table, except in a palace where rooms which are actually ballrooms or halls of mirrors are sometimes

pressed into service for dining. Elsewhere **chandeliers** may hang at any height at least high enough to clear the heads of the tallest men. If a chandelier is electrified, each individual bulb—even if it is a candle bulb—simply must be shaded or shielded from the eye and not left bare as a literally glaring error. Anyone who tells you that bulbs need not be shaded is undoubtedly trying to sell you a chandelier with bulbs that are not. Real candles are another thing; the flare and flicker and fade of firelight is always fascinating to look right at, and flattering to the audience too. No matter how tiny or Gargantuan the chandelier, as long as the diameter of the electrified candles is standard, shades must be two and a half to three inches in diameter at the top, three and a half to four and a half inches at the bottom, and three and a half to four and a half inches deep. Shades larger or smaller are wrong. Most are. All-crystal chandeliers require fabric shades; metal-and-crystal chandeliers, fabric or paper shades; tôle chandeliers, tôle shades—or paper ones carefully painted to look like tôle.

These days if you want a hard-surface floor with almost if not absolutely all the color variations and intricacies of design possible in a rug, you can have it with vinyl tile. Vinyl is marvelous; with a little patience and craft you can cut and fit it to create an inlaid leopard or flower garden or peacock. In a recent ram's-head design, I used eleven values of terra cotta alone. Vinyl lends itself to insertions of brass or steel or aluminum, though I certainly wouldn't ever use wood or ceramic inserts as some people do. Vinyl which attempts to imitate actual marble may get an A in Effort, but always an F in Verisimilitude. Vinyl impressionistically marbleized, the way it usually is on floors of so-called rumpus rooms, creates competition for any inlaid design. It by now may come as little surprise to you that **vinyl tile** floor must have a contrasting border, though in this case it may be a cove border which provides a self-baseboard and actually a service in being easy to clean. On a large expanse of floor, and of course except for the design or mosaic elements, thirty-inch squares are better than twelve-inch, and twelve-inch better than nine-inch, true both with checkerboard and solid treatments. Vinyl tile belongs on the floor, and not ascending the walls, as advertisements in decorating magazines would have you believe.

Napoleon and his senior officers spent a lot of time grubbing about in the field far from the painted salons of Paris, but took some comfort in the elegance (and indestructibility) of **206** the **steel furniture** they commissioned to take campaigning with them. Such furniture was either collapsible or dismantleable or both; was made by gunsmiths of gun metal; but was often designed by first-rate cabinet designers. These ébénistes immediately discovered that the greater strength of steel permitted bolder, more open silhouette, while inviting the elaborate and lacy treatment possible with wood. For some reason, perhaps simply because of its steelness, even the frilliest steel has a masculine and substantial look. Steel belongs particularly in a room in which its muted sheen can contrast with the soft warmth of wood or the lusciousness of silks, satins, and velvets. Steel furniture today is lacquered against rust, and need not be polished. Good antique steel is in curtailed supply, but at least not in the extreme demand it would be if the proletariat regarded it as suitable for anything other than yard or attic, and far too expensive for either one.

So many sculptors are hacking and chipping and casting away today that no one need content himself with copies any more; galleries groan under the weight of perfectly respectable although rarely downright admirable originals, at prices which **208** make possible two pieces of **sculpture** in every living room if not in every garage. Yet copies should not be airily dismissed. The top ten best-selling copies may wisely be bypassed —Queen Nefertiti, Le Penseur, the Statue of Liberty, et al., but copies of lesser-known masterpieces have arguments in their favor over original unmasterpieces. Copies don't have to be the same size as the original, nor of the same material. A marble statue, for example, could be copied with integrity in bronze, terra cotta, wood, stone, or papier mâché. However, proportion is vital, and copies which elongate or compress, or which modify, simplify, or change completely the detailing, should be smashed up or melted down as a public service. Studies appealing in the round may be mounted on bases which, like a lazy susan, can be rotated to bring all the goodies from time to time into view. I find mobiles distracting. They encourage intimation of personal inadequacy—I never know what to watch or where to look—which overcomes people at a three-ring circus. They seem rarely to be dusted properly.

The American housewife would as soon be caught without a sink in her kitchen or a bathtub in her bathroom as without a so-called coffee or cocktail table in front of the living-room sofa. These tables are usually long—sometimes almost as long as the sofa itself—and have the effect of barricading people on the sofa during parties. Large square and large round tables are a nuisance too because it takes so much time and effort to circumnavigate them. Much more satisfactory are **210** **small tables**, two to a sofa. Small antique benches of wood or metal, stripped of upholstery and with new marble tops, make ideal small tables. Tops may also be made from tôle trays, clear plate glass, lacquered wood, and panels from Chinese lacquered chests and doors. Small tables are also more useful than large ones because they may easily be moved about. They are satisfying to look at in front of the bulk of the sofa. No more than two tables should be used in any one group because three or more tables unavoidably seem to be marching.

What I call the comfort quotient of so-called (and aptly called) overstuffed upholstered seating has become exaggerated out of all relation to the facts. Which are that it's as comfortable to sit in more understuffed furniture and that it's easier to get in and out of it gracefully, as anyone knows who has watched a plump woman disengaging herself from the clutches of a low, deep and enveloping overstuffed chair. And so I **212** avoid **overupholstered furniture**, America's largest selling kind by far. I believe in trim neatly tailored chairs, and sofas of the same breed, often with a single simple cushion across entire back and seat, and never more than seven feet long because I don't like people strung along sofas like birds on a wire. Even three people on a sofa can be awkward because the head of the person playing center keeps getting in the way of the flow of conversation between left and right end. Bulk and capaciousness, then, do not actually produce an aura of greater hospitality, as is commonly believed, but lesser. And far better to keep all upholstered furniture up on legs at least one or two inches from the floor for float—except when a sofa fits exactly into a separate architectural area of a room, like a bay window or alcove, where it may be desirable to upholster to the floor to continue the effect of wall across the sofa without interruption. Foam rubber does not require fluffing. Down does. Foam is neat and trim but less lush. I suggest a combination of foam and down on upholstered seating for comfort and neatness, half and half.

214 The three kinds of **lamp shades** I use are: translucent fabric shades, usually silk; opaque paper shades, usually with hand-painted decorations; and tôle shades, usually antique. The French (and the American do-it-yourself) tendency is to overscale fabric and paper shades—to make them too tall and fat for the lamps themselves—and to underscale tôle shades. Clients who at first think the fabric and paper shades I choose are too small, almost invariably come to agree with the more pleasant scaling when they have lived with the lamps long enough to become conditioned to the power of understatement. I prefer opaque shades which direct light and eye to the presumably beautiful lamp base below, rather than translucent shades which focus attention upon the source of the light.

If your mother telephones with news that she's just bought an oriental rug, and doesn't elaborate, your fund of general information is little enriched, for oriental rugs are any rugs produced across an area including nearly half the circumference of the earth, from the Nile to the North China Sea. It could be Turkish or Chinese or Persian or Turkoman or Samarkand or on and on. And, aside from all having pile which is actually part of the backing, none of them has much in common with the others, e.g., Moslem ones have a definite direction of pattern the more totally to face Mecca with, while Samarkands worship general geometric order. Oriental rugs date from before the days of King Solomon, have been used successfully in western houses (where they fit into almost any conceivable scheme) since Marco Polo, and are of all grades from this side of worthless to the far side of precious; the designation oriental refers no more to quality than the designation Chicago would. Worn antique rugs can be more attractive than unworn ones as long as they aren't worn clear through. Only an expert full of scholarship can determine the true value of an antique oriental through minute examination of color, design, material, and workmanship, in this area where skulduggery is traditionally endemic. We've imitated **216** the various **oriental rugs** on power looms for more than a century, but the imitations are relatively odious. In common with all correct rugs, orientals always have a border.

I subscribe to few magazines because I do not like them to arrive folded or rolled, and instead buy them flat at the newsstand. Flatness is important since, depending of course upon the cover of the particular issue, magazines can be pleasant decorative accessories, just lying around. With some magazines, like *Punch* and the *New Yorker* and the old *Saturday Review,* you don't have to worry about the particular issue; all of them

218 look good anywhere. When lying loose, **magazines** should lie singly or in perpendicular stacks, with the prettiest and most harmonious on top, and should never be arranged in a stream with the title of each sticking out, the way they always are in clubs for septuagenarian men. Some satisfactory magazine racks which were designed as magazine racks exist, but most tasteful people more often than not prefer to bend jardinieres, decorative wastebaskets, wine coolers, or antique hat boxes to the purpose. Whether they are decorative or not, though, it is an omission not to include magazines in any setting where a guest might ever be waiting or bored or both.

When the fabric on an upholstered piece is forthright in both color and design, it is better not interfered with by pillows of contrasting fabric. But otherwise, pillows may—and should—provide flashes of color and texture against whatever upholstery they are placed. If I have a formula for pillows on sofas, which I haven't, it's often at least two pillows in one fabric and at least one other pillow in contrasting color and fabric. But there is actually no limit to the color and number of different kinds of pillows used on a chair or sofa so long as all colors evolve from the master scheme and there is still room to sit down. Pillows can be knife-edge (welted all around of course) or boxed. They can be round or rectangular or square, but never triangular. Different sizes, as well as different shapes, are pleasant on a given sofa. Foam rubber

220 pillows feel like upholstered gelatin; therefore **pillows** should always be down. Some may be trimmed with fringe or braid, or embroidered, for interest and elegance. One of the two do-it-yourself projects properly available to clients, when professionally advised, is the production of embroidery and needlepoint for pillows—the other is cutting out wallpaper borders—but there should never be so much that it suggests the output of a dedicated convent. In contemporary settings pillows are compulsory, because of their welcoming powers.

You can do practically anything with leather that you can with upholstery fabric, plus some things that you can't, such as tiling a floor with it. Leather is obviously more durable than fabric, doesn't fade as fast, and when it does fade does so attractively, with welcome unevenness. For upholstery and wall, door and curtain treatments, **leather** has but two disadvantages worth worrying about. First, that hides are just so big, and even though each contains about fifty square feet you can only use about three quarters of this because of the free-form shape. And second, because it is less pliable than fabric, leather is far harder to work with. Hides are usually sliced into four layers like veneers—top grain, deep buff, split, and sist—and the top grain is most difficult to use because it's toughest. Top grain also naturally has the most irregularities—scars and abrasions which are souvenirs of entanglements with barbed wire, etc.; but unless these accidents were spectacular they cause no more distress than imperfections in graining of wood would. Leather may be embossed or embellished with ornamented or blind tooling. I have success printing cornices and pilasters on leather walls.

Great fun (cutting them out), games (planning where they'll go), and results (living with them) are yours to be had with **224 wallpaper borders**. When a room has no picture molding or cornice you have no alternatives but to use a wallpaper border to stop the wallpaper at the ceiling, or to go ahead and paper the ceiling too. Sadly enough most people don't even know that they have no other choice. A crisp, tailored idea is to frame all four boundaries of each architecturally defined wall area in a room with border, automatically providing double borders at corners for a gratifying accent upon accent there. But more can be done with borders than bordering. Let me recapitulate a successful combination of wallpapers and borders in a single lovely room. The principal paper is vertically striped and runs from ceiling to chair rail. All striped areas are bordered with a paper border that looks like molding. At the ceiling, a paper-border frieze accomplishes the transition from wall to ceiling. The chair rail is another paper border, under which we have marbleized wallpaper for the dado, with panels on the dado created by moldings of contrasting marbleized paper border. And bottoming it all off is yet another contrasting marbleized border. Here seven papers and borders in all create in combination anything but the discordant effect you might on first hearing expect, and instead an almost intolerably tailored and restrained and elegant one. Here wallpaper has stood in for cornice, moldings, chair rail, dado, and baseboard and has turned out to be not the stand-in for all of them, but the star.

226 consoles are almost impossible to define; they're like tables, but with subtle little differences. They always stand against a wall (or against the back of a piece of furniture), sometimes supported by the wall and only two legs of their own, though they can have four. They are usually relatively thin for their length. And, though they may be put to some incidental use like collecting the mail in an entrance hall or displaying several ornaments none of which really has to be there, their primary role must be decorative rather than functional. The two tests for consolality are these. If you can walk all the way around it alone it's not a console because one side of a genuine console must abut on something else. And if it is not an end in itself, without performing other mandatory duties like being eaten off of or supporting necessary (as opposed to unnecessary) lamps, then it isn't a console either.

Round draped tables, a favorite in European settings since the Renaissance, didn't leap the Atlantic until the middle of the nineteenth century and just because the trip was merely coincidentally contemporaneous with Victoria's reign are to this day erroneously typed as Victorian by lightly probing minds. Depending of course upon what you drape them with, draped tables can be charming, dignified, self-effacing, or colorful and sometimes some places actually more desirable than any other kind of table. Though the frame or table underneath may have cost an unheady $3.98, draped tables are hardly a make-do economy, for they all but demand the use of the most lavish antique brocades or other costly fabrics, and require no less than five yards of fifty-inch material, plus eight yards of braid or fringe if applied only in a single tier around the circumference of the skirt, for a table thirty inches in diameter. If not pleated for tailored restraint, in which case it should barely caress the floor so as not to discommode the pleats, the fabric must break on the floor to form a demi-pouf of rich bouffant fullness. Hence unless pleated, **draped tables** are characteristically soft. I have used felt and leather for draping tables in bachelor apartments, but otherwise a draped table implies a female lurking somewhere about the house.

228

Probably no word in the decorating lexicon has been so maligned and misapplied as provincial. Walk onto the furniture **230** floor of any department store and ask to see a **provincial** piece and you will surely be shown something derivative (although sometimes remotely) from Louis XV. Now of course it is true that there was provincial furniture of the period of Louis XV, but it is also true that there was provincial furniture produced during every other period since the Pleistocene, including Empire. Provincial furniture is simply any furniture which happened to be made in the country, as opposed to town, during any period whatsoever. Provincial furniture is usually less ornamented, less sophisticated, less meticulously finished, less "pure," and often more charming and guileless than unprovincial furniture, but only a furniture salesman would tell you that provincial can be recognized by line or silhouette, for these are always true to whatever period. Unfortunately, this is exactly what all the furniture salesmen have told all America, and they have been believed.

Oddly enough, you can often get more decorative traction out of stools and benches than you can from chairs. Except for not being able to lean back on them you can put them to exactly the same use as chairs, and because their presence is less obtrusive they can be attractively positioned in more places, including the middle of the room, without impeding visual or pedal traffic. When placed under large tables or desks they can still be seen while using up no floor space at all. Their portability is another gold star on their chart, and if they are upholstered in incisive accent colors (like many pillows) they provide pleasant and varying color juxtapositions wherever in the room they may momentarily turn up. Pairs of benches look especially good when they are posed side by side; the cluster of little legs creates an interesting silhouette. Antique benches graciously allow some of their respectability to rub off on whatever's put on top of them when they are used as tables; here's a way to help make a small television set look legitimate, though just to help. Ottomans, the heavier upholstered relatives of benches, serve separately as an extra seat or, in combination with an upholstered armchair, make the armchair into a chaise longue which isn't as inflexible as an actual chaise longue. I use **stools and benches** as frequently as impromptu tables as I do as stools and benches. Rather than go through the ritual of moving the (carefully arranged) still life of objects from my bedside table every morning and then putting it back, I always have my breakfast tray placed on a stool brought to the bed for the purpose.

232

234 The best thing about **stripes** is that they can go up and down for always precious verticality. Stripes almost can't help but look fresh and crisp and tailored, but best of all they can, when they're run up the walls and then mitred on the ceiling, make a tent room, which everybody from the age of three up adores being in. Thin stripes can be more feminine and bold ones more masculine, but if you can circumvent banking on it, do. Striped fabrics tend to make fat upholstered pieces look thinner, true as well of people. Narrower stripes belong on smaller pieces, and bolder on larger, because, obviously, bold stripes overwhelm small pieces and narrow stripes lose their footing on large. I enjoy lining the most elegant and expensive damask and silk taffeta draperies in an incidental narrow striped cotton, and bringing the lining around to the fore as a border, provided the fabric being so lined and bordered is plain. Marie Antoinette liked to do this too. Striped floors come off well when the stripes are used to make a narrow room seem wider by running at right angles to the axis. The same is true of ceilings. Stripes in the form of bands finish off the bottoms of lamp shades, provide admirable borders for almost any conceivable flat thing like rugs, and are, in short, or long, generically satisfactory. Stripes—like Mozart quintets—improve almost any situation. Besides, they can make the surroundings narrower or wider or higher or lower or anything. Stripes are putty in your designer's hands.

People are fond of elevating their noses at veneer. Yet only use of carefully chosen and matched veneers makes possible all but identical graining repeats across a sweep of boiserie. The quantity of paneling to be used in a room should govern the choice of graining or vice versa: the more dramatic the wood the less of it there can be and the greater simplicity of design required. Woods with any persistent patterning at all should never be used to panel a room entirely. They should be reserved to create a more local focal point of interest. Though every design period expressed itself differently and characteristically in boiserie, all concurred that you can't have a limitless expanse of uninterrupted wood surface and must divide it up into sections within itself. The English ran to horizontal paneling within the paneling, the French to vertical; I'm with vertical and the French. Direction of graining must always correspond to the direction of axis of a component wood part, always true of all wood-finished wood everywhere. Stock lumber lengths should be avoided when designing **236 boiserie** because they invariably inhibit the design. Painted wood paneling enjoys a vogue today because it costs less now than to mold in plaster. Plywood, like veneer, is not a dirty word; over the long stretch plywood is far less likely to warp; some of my most elegant boiseries are plywood and veneer combined. Wood paneling can be relieved with glass, steel, wire, tooled leather, fabric, marble, lacquer, brass, or almost anything else hard and longevous that comes to mind.

In the eighteenth century the term used for lacquering was japanning with a little j. It could just as easily have been chineseing with a little c. The three most universally admired gifts of the orient, Japan and China, to the west are silk, porcelain, and lacquer. Besides lacquer, the ingredient essential to the entirely texture-free look of translucent color-in-depth of fine lacquer ware is patience. Quality derives from how many layers of lacquer are applied and how carefully and thoroughly each layer is hand-rubbed down to eliminate any hint of graining or, in the case of clear lacquer, to dramatize the graining beneath a flawlessly smooth surface. Satisfactory lacquer spraying machines exist, but to this day the best machine for rubbing ever invented has five fingers. Mottling or marbleizing the lacquer complicates the lacquerer's life further than plain. Colors springing before the mind's eye at the mention of lacquer are black and Chinese red, but of **238** course **lacquer** can be any other color also, and sometimes more interesting if it is. Some Chinese glazes, like mirror black, impart the look of lacquer to porcelain.

Many interior designers impose their will adamantly upon their clients in the selection and placement of pictures. I do not. Pictures are like underwear—so personal a matter that an interior designer, like an underwear salesman, has no business doing more than gently advising which picture and where. Rooms are often "done around" pictures. This is all right, but in some of my rooms hang **pictures** which were commissioned to be "done around" the otherwise completed room, in precisely matched colors. In other words, if you must have the "done around" look, you can do it backwards successfully and sometimes better. It is not always desirable to frame pictures, or to center them on wall or panel, or to hang them at all. Sometimes illumination is more effective when pictures stand on the floor and lean against a wall or piece of furniture. Such flagrant informality contributes an interest of its own. I never use individual picture lights, fastened to the frame, to light pictures because the light is too harsh and the pictures look for sale. Pin-point lighting from the ceiling often gives the unpleasant impression that pictures have been painted on glass and are being lit from the rear. Portraits of the lady of the house should probably not be hung in rooms where entertaining occurs, since they invite disastrous comparisons between fancy and fact, or what once was and now is.

242 daybeds are the same as sofabeds and sofabeds are never never the same as those revolting fold-up contraptions, made to spill forth their innards at night in a tangle of lumpy engineering, which have simply committed grand larceny by stealing the name. Any nonfolding, noncollapsing, or nondisappearing bed thirty-six inches or less wide becomes a daybed when pillows, leaning against the wall, provide the sofa back, with bolsters at either end usually filling in as arms. The mistake the misguided make is to attempt to create a daybed out of raw material more than thirty-six inches wide, for it can't be done. If you insist on trying, what you get is a bed with various pillows on it but not a daybed, which, subtracting the depth of its pillow back, can't be too deep to sit back all the way on without your legs sticking out in the air. In daybeds, the difference between thirty-six and thirty-nine inches is total (and more than thirty-nine inches a country mile). With a thirty inch width, one finds the bed narrow enough for the most natural sitting and still (barely) wide enough for comfortable sleeping. All this enforced narrowness makes daybeds wonderful space savers for small rooms, or for that matter big rooms. My favorites are ones with metal legs, frames, and ends because they are more open and elegant and usually less beddy than wood or upholstered jobs. Regardless of the width, if your daybed doesn't look more like a sofa or settee than a bed, then face it, you have a bed.

Shower curtains should be as meticulously designed and trimmed as window curtains. In small bathrooms where two unrelated curtain ideas wouldn't have elbow room, shower curtains and window curtains should match. If the tub or shower area is attractive, as it is probably not, two curtains are better than one; they can be tied back with tiebacks, one on each side to frame the tub. If the installation is ugly, or if there are those depressing frosted-glass doors, the shower curtain should be on twenty-four hour decorative duty and remain drawn across the area. Curtains which flow from ceiling to floor introduce an opulence appealing in bathrooms because you've been conditioned by most bathrooms to expect spare and bare function and frugality. Lavishness in the bathroom is such a pleasant surprise that I often make the shower curtains out of startlingly luxurious fabrics. Transparent plastic exists in sheets large enough to serve as a waterproof lining to the decorative curtain, and if the lining is attached only at the top, the decorative curtain may remain outside the tub while the bottom of the lining is at work inside. Particularly in newer buildings, bathrooms are often little architectural monstrosities—a tangle of odd beam ends, weirdly dimensioned surfaces, sunken ceilings, and capriciously located windows, if **244** any. Here **shower curtains**, often with the help of valances, can cover a multitude of sins and provide an illusion of order and purpose to architecture which possesses neither.

The Frenchman's favorite period—and the one which suffers innocently and mistakenly throughout America's furniture stores as the prototype of "provincial"—is Louis XV. Maybe

246 the French like it so much because **louis xv** reigned for so long a time, or maybe because there's consequently so much of it that they just see it more and are more used to it. Louis XV, which might more aptly be named Pompadour I, was the essence of freely drawn rococo, all of it erected upon the ubiquitous cabriole leg. Without the cabriole Louis XV wouldn't literally have had a leg to stand on. Being freely drawn, no two cabrioles are quite alike (except on the same piece of furniture or in the same suite), but all have a severe curve toward the top and a gentler one toward the bottom. Backs and arms of things were freely drawn curves too. This was the most feminine of French periods—Empire was to be the most masculine—and continues as the foolproof period in which to do a woman's bedroom if not her house. Pompadour's taste, charm, and intelligence were everywhere. Everything she touched became lovely and, as perhaps the greatest patroness of the arts ever, she touched very nearly everything.

Some immigrants from English pottery works came to the French town of Creil-sur-Oise at the end of the eighteenth century where, for a hundred years, they and their successors produced Creil, perhaps the most appealing soft-paste glazed pottery in the world. Then, suddenly (and briefly), the market lost interest in Creil, the factory fell into decline and decay, and the recipe died with the last potter, never to be duplicated since. Creil is therefore doomed to utter extinction and becomes rarer by the year as accidents befall individual members of the Creil population. Creil was to the provincial table what Sèvres was to the patrician; Creil was cheaper and less elegant but blessed with more character and with a distinctive and deceptive lighter-than-it-looks heft. Ground colors are usually three: water green, which is far rarer than bright butter yellow, which is far rarer than white, relatively rare to begin with. All were ornamented with black stencil designs, sometimes subjects in series like the months of the year or military heroes or even balloon ascensions; each ground color was occasionally decorated in its own palette of other colors too. My conviction is that the finer things in life, one of which is Creil, should be in day to day utilitarian use and not left shut up in cabinets like museum collections, heartbreaking though it **248** is to see a service of **creil** gradually dwindle away as the years swing on and take their toll. The only reason for ownership of things is to live with them in continuous intimacy, and if they have to gradually pass on, alas, but so too do we.

Some hostesses darken the dining room even for luncheon so candles can be used. Daytime or nighttime, people look more attractive by candlelight, and especially while eating, when they are put to the acid test of meeting sustained and narrow scrutiny without being able to move about or excessively animate themselves. An accurate measure of the degree of importance a hostess attaches to a given party is the number of **250 candles** she has burning simultaneously; a gathering lit exclusively and entirely by candles is all but doomed for success. It's a pity that faces look even better when candlelit from below than above, because the height of most candles combined with the height of whatever holder is holding them make such underlighting impossible. The original before-lit height of a candle really should not exceed the height of the candelabrum, unless there is advance reason to believe that the evening will be a protracted one. I always like to use candles in chandeliers in dining rooms, sometimes in drawing rooms, and never in bedrooms. Cylindrical candles are preferable to tapered ones because they look prettier both burning and not burning. Candles in sconces in narrow foyers and hallways create a traffic problem, and here, as in bedroom chandeliers, should be electrified. Colored candles—which include all but white, ivory, or natural tallow ones—should be summarily melted down for, possibly, industrial purposes.

Just as in the army it is customary either to salute, bury, or paint everything, in the eighteenth and nineteenth centuries it was fashionable to marbleize it. Hordes dabbed with their feathers marbleizing everything in sight and many things not, like end papers of books and insides of trunks. Today there is not so much of it being done, yet marbleizing has its secure role in contemporary decoration. Either literal or sketchy-impressionist renderings of actual marble are acceptable. Both may either be painted directly onto the area being treated or first painted on paper which is then applied. The Italians and French sometimes appear to have indulged themselves in flamboyant interpretations of marble the likes of which were never quarried; yet often we have never seen real marble like a given piece of antique marbleizing simply because the small exotic quarry the model marble came from has long since exhausted itself. Marbleizing must always be handled as real

252   marble would be. The **marbleizing** should appear "cut" and "fitted" in the form of logical marble shapes. You can't very well have a twenty-foot slab of real marble, so you shouldn't have a twenty-foot slab of marbleizing. There can't be perfect matches at joints. Horizontal panels should be marbleized horizontally and vertical vertically. In marbleizing door trim the top member should run straight across to the outside edges of the vertical members, and temptation to miter these joints should be resisted. Marbleizing is as high on the hog as genuine marble—if executed and used correctly.

On walls the same rules govern upholstery as on furniture: the fabric must be finished at the edges with either gimp or nailheads or single self-welt. In addition, any doors which fall within an upholstered area, which one wishes didn't, should be finished with hand-sewn piping to interrupt the flow of the fabric as little as possible. An upholstered room looks more totally conceived when the curtains are of material identical to that on the walls, an impression further enhanced when an important piece of furniture is upholstered in this fabric as

254 well. Actually, correctly **upholstered walls** are double upholstered, for in any craftsmanlike job walls must first be lined with flannel. You can use anything you want to upholster wall from denim to damask. Because the cost of the workmanship to upholster the walls of a room properly is so paralyzing, some people go out of their way to use inexpensive fabrics as a kind of reverse status symbol. But this has no bearing on the decorative effect which is good or bad simply depending upon the specific fabric, cheap or dear.

acknowledgments

There are 124 photographs in this book. Credit with my warm thanks is due as follows: 2—Good Housekeeping magazine; 5—reprinted from Vogue, copyright © 1957 by The Conde-Nast Publications, Inc., photographed by Andre Kertesz; 7—Eastman Chemical Products, Inc., and Mr. Charlton Heston; 12—Johns Manville Sales Corporation, photographed by Hans Van Nes; 13—reprinted from House & Garden, copyright © 1954 by The Conde-Nast Publications, Inc.; 14—reprinted from Vogue, copyright © 1957 by The Conde-Nast Publications, Inc., photographed by Andre Kertesz; 21—New York Times Studio; 22—Johns-Manville Sales Corporation, photographed by Hans Van Nes; 23—Katzenbach & Warren; 24—Interior Decorators News, photographed by Ernest Silva; 26—reprinted from Vogue, copyright © 1957 by The Conde-Nast Publications, Inc., photographed by Andre Kertesz; 43—reprinted from Vogue, copyright © 1957 by The Conde-Nast Publications, Inc.; 46—National Society of Interior Designers, River York House, reproduced from McCall's magazine, photographed by Louis Reens; 52—reprinted from Interiors, copyright by Whitney Publications Inc., photographed by Ernest Silva; 57—Town & Country magazine, photographed by Hans Van Nes; 74—Midtown Galleries, photographed by Ernest Silva; 76—New York Times Studio; 85—American Fabrics Magazine; 91—New York Herald Tribune; 100—reprinted from Vogue, copyright © 1959 by The Conde-Nast Publications, Inc., photographed by Tom Leonard; 104—Grosfeld House; 108—Upholstery Leather Group, room photographed by Ernest Silva at the Midtown Galleries. Painting by Emlen Etting; 110—Antiques Magazine, photographed by Taylor & Dull; 115—reprinted from Interior Design, photographed by James Vincent; 118—reprinted from Vogue, copyright © 1957, by The Conde-Nast Publications, Inc., photographed by Andre Kertesz; 119—Owens-Corning-Fiberglas* Corporation; 120—reprinted from Interior Design, photographed by James Vincent; all other photographs by Ernest Silva.

I also wish to thank the following publications in which other photographs of rooms illustrated in this book originally appeared: *American Fabrics Magazine, American Home, The American Weekly, Antiques,* Atlanta *Journal & Constitution,* Bartow *Democrat,* Bay City *Times, Better Homes & Gardens, Bride's Magazine, Building Supply News, Christian Science Monitor,* Columbus *Dispatch, Contract Magazine,* Daytona Beach *News Journal,* Detroit *News, The Diplomat, Everywoman's Family Circle, Floor Covering Weekly,* Gary *Post-Tribune, Gentleman's Quarterly,* Greenfield *Recorder-Gazette,* Greenville *News, Home Furnishings Daily, House Beautiful, Interior Decorators News, Interior Design, Interiors, Life,* Long Island *Press, Look,* Los Angeles *Sunday Pictorial Magazine,* Medina *Gazette,* Newark *News,* Newark *Star-Ledger,* New York *Daily News,* New York *Herald Tribune,* New York *Journal American,* New York *Times,* New York *World Telegram & Sun, Newsday, Parade,* Philadelphia *Bulletin,* Philadelphia *Inquirer,* Plainfield *Courier-News,* St. Petersburg *Times, Scrantonian,* Spokane *Spokesman Review, Today's Home Decorating Guide, This Week,* Toledo *Blade, Trentonian,* Washington *Post,* Washington *Star,* Wilkes-Barre *Times-Leader-News, Be Your Own Decorator* and *Guide to Interior Decoration,* by Betty Pepis, Emily Post's *Etiquette.*

In addition, of course, my even warmer thanks go to clients who made the work shown here possible in the first place: Mr. and Mrs. Harry Anholt; Miss Barbara Bishop; Mr. and Mrs. Wingate Bixby; Mr. and Mrs. Arthur Blakemore; Mr. and Mrs. Robert Brooks; Mrs. Grace Buck; Mr. and Mrs. Joseph N. Carpenter; Mr. and Mrs. Edgar Cullman; Miss Kay Daly; Mrs. Joseph Dombroff; Miss Stephanie Edgell; Mrs. Lincoln Ellsworth; Mr. and Mrs. Richard Ernst; Lord and Lady Essendon; Mr. and Mrs. Howeth Townsend Ford; Mr. and Mrs. George Franklin; Mr. and Mrs. R. W. Freeman; Mr. and Mrs. George E. George; Mr. and Mrs. Milton A. Gordon; Mr. and Mrs. Ira Guilden; Mr. and Mrs. Richard Halliday (Mrs. Halliday is the actress Mary Martin); Colonel and Mrs. Stedman Shumway Hanks; Mr. and Mrs. Waldo Hatch; Mr. Charlton Heston; Mrs. George Hutzler; Mr. and Mrs. Oliver Iselin, Jr.; Mr. Alan Koehler; Miss Barbara Kraus; Mr. and Mrs. Peter I. B. Lavan; Mr. and Mrs. Charles C. Lawrence; Mr. and Mrs. Rensselaer W. Lee; Mr. and Mrs. Isaac Marcosson; Mr. and Mrs. O. E. McIntyre; Mr. Donald McVay; Mr. and Mrs. Arnold Michaelis; Mrs. William B. Olmsted, Jr.; Mr. and Mrs. Edward A. O'Neal; Miss Geraldine Page; Mr. and Mrs. C. Jay Parkinson; Mr. and Mrs. Ezra Prentice; Mr. and Mrs. Willard Ray (Mrs. Ray is the author, Marie Beynon Ray); Mr. and Mrs. Herbert H. Rogge; Mr. James C. Ryan; Mr. Michael St. Clair; Mr. and Mrs. Seymour Schweber; Mrs. Edward G. Sparrow; Miss Barbara Thurston; Mr. and Mrs. Olin Tice; Mr. and Mrs. Henry McD. Tichenor; Mrs. C. E. G. Tuthill; Mrs. Henry H. Wehrhane; Mr. and Mrs. Peter Wehrli; Mr. and Mrs. Theodore Weicker, Jr.; Mr. and Mrs. A. Weinberg; Mr. and Mrs. Walter Werner.

Further, I wish to express special gratitude to those clients in public (and private) life who permitted their property to be photographed and reproduced even though they personally insist upon their inalienable right of privacy to the degree that they wish not to be identified here.